BTRIPP BOOKS

BOOK REVIEWS FROM

2004-6

BY BRENDAN TRIPP

*These reviews originally appeared on the
"BTRIPP'S BOOKS" book review blog:
http://btripp-books.livejournal.com/*

Copyright © 2016 by Brendan Tripp

ISBN 978-1-57353-406-2

An Eschaton Book

http://www.EschatonBooks.com

Front cover photo courtesy Kenn W. Kiser via morguefile.com.
Back cover photo courtesy Sebastian Santana via morguefile.com.

PREFACE

From 1993 through 2004, I ran the *first* manifestation of Eschaton Books (now in its third revival). Initially started as a vehicle to publish my poetry, it soon became evident that the market for poetry is vanishingly small, and in 1994 it "pivoted" into being a metaphysical press.

In this time, I was largely a one-man shop, doing everything from editorial to shipping, which was a huge time commitment, and I typically worked 14 hour days, 7 days a week to keep things moving. I bring up all this here because, despite having been a life-long avid reader, during this period I had precious little time for reading, and what reading I *did* get done was largely assessing book submissions. However, I never stopped *buying* books, which began to stack up in prodigious "to be read" piles.

When Eschaton went out of business in 2004 (in a sadly not unusual denouement for a small press – we had a distributor who ended up never paying us, while selling through all our stock), I found myself with a lot of books to catch up on, and a need to keep my writing chops sharp. So, I began to pen little reviews of what I was reading, and post those on the web.

As the years went by, this became "a thing" that I was doing, and, for a while, I was targeting a fairly aggressive goal of getting at least 72 non-fiction books read per year. By 2015, this had resulted in my having read and reviewed 700 books over that 12-year span.

In recent years (since the upswing in print-on-demand publishing), I have had numerous acquaintances suggest that I put out my reviews as books. I was, at first, rather hesitant on the concept (as, after all, the material was free to read on the web), but I eventually figured that if various people who were *not* me thought it was a good idea, I might as well give it a shot.

I started with the most recent reviews, those from 2015, and worked backwards. This is the tenth of these collections, with the reviews from 2004, 2005, and 2006, representing the time that I was "getting up to speed" with the reviews. It's a truism for writers that it's often very painful to look back on one's old copy from a later context, and this is certainly the case here, a decade and more down the line. Most notably "painful" is the vast number of these that are titled "Another Book" ... but I do have a defense for this irritating artifact. In 2004-6 there were very few social media platforms, and I *lived* on LiveJournal, which typically saw many posts from me a day, pretty much every day. The book reviews were showing up in that stream, and were getting noted as being, well, "hey, here's another book I read". As my text got spread across other services, the "novelty" of a book review appearing faded, so later reviews featured headers more about the book in question rather than the simple fact of it being a review.

Also, my early reviews were very short compared to my more recent output, and some of the ones here hardly classify *as* reviews. There are quite a lot of them here, however, with a whopping 105 books covered (more, if you count those just name-checked in the introductory post). Again, I can hardly consider this my "best work", but it was my take on these titles as I read them back in the day (and I'm glad I eventually gave up on trying to *write* the reviews in the same order I finished *reading* the books - OCD can be a real hassle at times!).

As noted in previous intros, I do not write classic reviews, but more a telling of my personal interaction with a particular book. This means that I talk about where and how I got the book, how it relates to other things I've read, what reactions it triggered in me (and why), and how one can get a copy if it sounds appealing. I recently read a biography of Hunter S. Thompson, and noted some similarity in my reviewing style to how his "journalistic style" was being described ... but I'm not sure I'm ready to try to assume the mantle of "Gonzo". Needless to say, if the reader is devoted to "standard" book reviewing styles, this might be an irritation ... however, it does make these reviews somewhat idiosyncratic to *me*, resulting in this series of collections being something of a "my encounters with books" sort of deal, which will, hopefully, be of interest to many readers.

- Brendan Tripp

CONTENTS

v - Preface

vii - Contents

1 - **2004**

3 - Wednesday, February 4, 2004

books ...
{Introductory Post}
{various books/authors}

4 - Sunday, February 22, 2004

Book ...
Zen Physics:
The Science of Death, the Logic of Reincarnation
by David J. Darling

5 - Friday, February 27, 2004

Another book ...
The Tao of Pooh
by Benjamin Hoff

6 - Friday, March 5, 2004

another book ...
The Te of Piglet
by Benjamin Hoff

7 - Tuesday, March 9, 2004

more books ...
Treason: Liberal Treachery
from the Cold War to the War on Terrorism
by Ann Coulter

9 - Monday, March 15, 2004

Buy this book! BUY THIS BOOK!
Slander: Liberal Lies About the American Right
by Ann Coulter

10 - Friday, March 19, 2004

Another book ...
Breaking the Maya Code
by Michael D. Coe

12 - Saturday, March 27, 2004

Another book ...
The Light at the Edge of the Universe: Leading Cosmologists on the Brink of a Scientific Revolution
by Michael D. Lemonick

13 - Tuesday, April 6, 2004

Cool book!
All The Trouble In The World: The Lighter Side of Overpopulation, Famine, Ecological Disaster, Ethnic Hatred, Plague, and Poverty
by P.J. O'Rourke

14 - Friday, April 9, 2004

A BRILLIANT BOOK!
God Is Red: A Native View of Religion
by Vine Deloria, Jr.

16 - Tuesday, April 13, 2004

It's a classic ...
Neuromancer
by William Gibson

17 - Thursday, April 22, 2004

Another good book!
Parliament of Whores: A Lone Humorist Attempts to Explain the Entire U.S. Government
by P.J. O'Rourke

18 - Wednesday, May 5, 2004

another book ...
The Edges of Science: Crossing the Boundary from Physics to Metaphysics
by Richard Morris

20 - Thursday, May 20, 2004

Another book down ...
Cosmic Coincidences:
Dark Matter, Mankind, and Anthropic Cosmology
by John Gribbin & Martin Rees

22 - Monday, May 24, 2004

Bad Craziness ...
Songs of the Doomed:
More Notes on the Death of the American Dream
by Dr. Hunter S. Thompson

23 - Thursday, September 23, 2004

Another book ...
Why the Reckless Survive:
And Other Secrets of Human Nature
by Melvin Konner

25 - **2005**

27 - Wednesday, January 5, 2005

Another book ...
Fork It Over: The Intrepid Adventures
of a Professional Eater
by Alan Richman

28 - Monday, January 10, 2005

oh, lookie ... another book!
The Lost Ship of Noah: In Search of the Ark at Ararat
by Charles Berlitz

29 - Thursday, March 24, 2005

Woot ... finally finished one of these books!
The Essential Kabbalah:
The Heart of Jewish Mysticism
by Daniel C. Matt

30 - Monday, April 4, 2005

Finally ...
Universes
by John Leslie

31 - Wednesday, April 6, 2005

Well, that sure was different ...
Bible Code II: The Countdown
by Michael Drosnin

33 - Monday, April 11, 2005

Oh, boy ... quick reads are so refreshing!
The Mythology of North America
by John Bierhorst

34 - Sunday, April 24, 2005

Well, that's two out of three ...
The Mythology of South America
by John Bierhorst

35 - Wednesday, July 27, 2005

Whew ... that took a while ...
The Mythology of Mexico and Central America
by John Bierhorst

36 - Monday, September 5, 2005

And now for something completely different ...
Weird Illinois
by Troy Taylor

37 - Thursday, October 27, 2005

Finally done with this one ...
**Voices Of The First Day:
Awakening In The Aboriginal Dreamtime**
by Robert Lawlor

39 - Sunday, November 20, 2005

Another one bites the dust ...
**You Are the World: An Authentic Report of
Talks and Discussions in American Universities**
by J. Krishnamurti

40 - Wednesday, November 23, 2005

A small book ...
When The Sun Moves Northward: The Way Of Initiation
by Mabel Collins

41 - Tuesday, November 29, 2005

Another fast read ...
Creative Visualization: Use the Power of Your Imagination to Create What You Want in Your Life
by Shakti Gawain

42 - Tuesday, November 29, 2005

why, lookie there!
The Dervishes Of Turkey
by Lucy M.J. Garnett

44 - Saturday, December 17, 2005

Another book down ...
Voices Of Our Ancestors: Cherokee Teachings from the Wisdom Fire
by Dhyani Ywahoo

46 - Tuesday, December 20, 2005

A quick read ...
Eduardo El Curandero: The Words of a Peruvian Healer
by Eduardo Calderon & Douglas Sharon

48 - Friday, December 23, 2005

Another fast read ...
The Dead Sea Scrolls: After Forty Years
by Hershel Shanks

50 - Monday, December 26, 2005

Another book ... one EVERYBODY should check out!
Unfit For Command: Swift Boat Veterans Speak Out Against John Kerry
by John E. O'Neill & Jerome R. Corsi

52 - Thursday, December 29, 2005

Another book ...
Get In The Van: On The Road With Black Flag
by Henry Rollins

54 - Thursday, December 29, 2005

The quickest sort of read ...
**A Preliminary Edition Of The Unpublished
Dead Sea Scrolls: The Hebrew And Aramaic Texts
From Cave Four - Fascicle One**
by Ben Zion Wacholder

55 - **2006**

57 - Monday, January 9, 2006

Another book ...
**At the Heart of the Web:
The Inevitable Genesis of Intelligent Life**
by George A. Seielstad

59 - Monday, January 23, 2006

WOOT! ... finally finished this one!
Jesus & the Riddle of the Dead Sea Scrolls
by Barbara Thiering

61 - Friday, January 27, 2006

Another book ...
**Reading the Mind of God:
In Search of the Principle of Universality**
by James Trefil

63 - Sunday, February 5, 2006

Another book ...
Stones, Bones, and Ancient Cities
by Lawrence H. Robbins

64 - Thursday, February 9, 2006

Book ...
The Pagan Book of Days
by Nigel Pennick

65 - Monday, February 13, 2006

A Superb Book ...
Sufi Thought and Action
by Idries Shah

67 - Wednesday, February 15, 2006

A short read ...
Urban Legends and the Japanese Tale
by David Schaefer

68 - Thursday, February 16, 2006

A long time coming ...
**A Global Ethic: The Declaration
of the Parliament of the World's Religions**
by Hans Kung & Karl-Josef Kuschel

70 - Friday, February 17, 2006

A very silly book ...
The Art of Napping
by William A. Anthony

71 - Sunday, February 19, 2006

A strange little book ...
**Mount Analogue: A Novel of Symbolically Authentic
Non-Euclidean Adventures in Mountain Climbing**
by Rene Daumal

72 - Tuesday, February 21, 2006

another book ...
**Cultural Encounters: Essays on the Interactions
of Diverse Cultures Now and in the Past**
by Robert Cecil & David Wade, eds.

74 - Saturday, February 25, 2006

A trip down memory lane ...
Archaeological Mexico
by Marcia Castro Leal

75 - Wednesday, March 1, 2006

Another book ...
Lost Kingdoms of the Maya
by Gene S. Stuart & George E. Stuart

76 - Saturday, March 11, 2006

Hey, I did get something read these past few weeks!
Sacred Architecture
by A.T. Mann

78 - Tuesday, March 14, 2006

Another one bites the dust ...
**The Secret Language of Symbols :
A Visual Key to Symbols and Their Meanings**
by David Fontana

80 - Tuesday, March 21, 2006

An interesting read ...
**Magick, Shamanism & Taoism:
The I Ching in Ritual and Meditation**
by Richard Herne

82 - Sunday, March 26, 2006

Another book ...
**Kingdoms of Gold, Kingdoms of Jade:
The Americas Before Columbus**
by Brian M. Fagan

84 - Saturday, March 30, 2006

One last one for March ...
The New Archaeology and the Ancient Maya
by Jeremy A. Sabloff

85 - Saturday, April 1, 2006

Sorta taking a break ...
A Book of Angels
by Sophy Burnham

86 - Sunday, April 2, 2006

Yuck ...
Angel Letters
by Sophy Burnham

88 - Monday, April 3, 2006

That's more like it ...
The Gospel of Thomas: The Hidden Sayings of Jesus
by Marvin Meyer

90 - Thursday, April 6, 2006

Wow ...
**Native American History: A Chronology of a Culture's
Vast Achievements and Their Links to World Events**
by Judith Nies

91 - Thursday, April 13, 2006

Three small books ...
Easy Field Guide to Southwestern Petroglyphs
by Elizabeth C. Welsh
Easy Field Guide to Indian Art & Legends of the Southwest
by James R. Cunkle
Easy Field Guide to Rock Art Symbols of the Southwest
by Rick Harris

93 - Sunday, April 16, 2006

What interesting timing ...
Children of Kali: Through India in Search of Bandits, the Thug Cult, and the British Raj
by Kevin Rushby

95 - Sunday, April 23, 2006

NOT a quick read this time ...
Meister Eckhart: A Modern Translation
by Raymond B. Blakney

97 - Thursday, April 27, 2006

Interesting ...
The Constitution of the United States
by Harold J. Spaeth

99 - Wednesday, May 3, 2006

an odd read ...
Pagan Celtic Ireland: The Enigma of the Irish Iron Age
by Barry Raftery

100 - Thursday, May 4, 2006

Much better ...
Crazy Clouds: Zen Radicals, Rebels & Reformers
by Perle Besserman & Manfred Steger

101 - Sunday, May 7, 2006

A fascinating little book ...
King, Warrior, Magician, Lover: Rediscovering the Archetypes of the Mature Masculine
by Robert Moore & Douglas Gillette

103 - Tuesday, May 9, 2006

Fascinating ...
Tao Te Ching:
The Classic Book of Integrity and the Way by Lao Tzu
by Victor H. Mair

105 - Sunday, May 14, 2006

Some poetry (not mine) ...
Stranger Music: Selected Poems and Songs
by Leonard Cohen

107 - Monday, May 15, 2006

The first of three ...
The UFO Experience: A Scientific Inquiry
by J. Allen Hynek

109 - Friday, June 9, 2006

Here's number two ...
The Most Haunted House in England:
Ten Years' Investigation of Borley Rectory
by Harry Price

111 - Friday, June 9, 2006

While I'm at it ...
Hidden Channels of the Mind
by Louisa E. Rhine

113 - Monday, June 12, 2006

Nothing like old predictions ...
The Road Ahead
by Bill Gates

115 - Thursday, June 15, 2006

(heavy sigh) ... this one hit home ...
Between Bites: Memoirs of a Hungry Hedonist
by James Villas

117 - Wednesday, June 28, 2006

Oh, look ... a book!
The Celts: Europe's People of Iron
by Dale M. Brown, Ed.

118 - Thursday, June 29, 2006

and, another book ...
Aztecs: Reign of Blood and Splendor
by Dale M. Brown, Ed.

119 - Sunday, July 9, 2006

or, "Dude, Where's My Car?" by any other name ...
The Search For El Dorado
by Dale M. Brown, Ed.

120 - Thursday, July 13, 2006

The last of these ...
Egypt: Land of the Pharaohs
by Dale M. Brown, Ed.

121 - Friday, July 14, 2006

Yeah, another one ...
Ancient Egypt
by John Baines & Jaromir Malek

123 - Saturday, July 15, 2006

Wow ...
Adventures in Afghanistan
by Louis Palmer

125 - Tuesday, July 18, 2006

Hmmmmm ...
**My Life: From Brigand to King
-- Auto-biography of Amir Habibullah**
by Amir Habibullah & Jamal Gul

127 - Friday, July 21, 2006

Another odd one ...
My Khyber Marriage
by Morag Murray Abdulah

129 - Sunday, July 30, 2006

Well, that's more like it!
Afghan Caravan
by Safia Shah, Ed.

131 - Tuesday, August 1, 2006

And now for something completely different ...
Why Ireland Never Invaded America
by Conor Cunneen

132 - Wednesday, August 9, 2006

A bit of a longer read ...
Prehistoric Mesoamerica
by Richard E.W. Adams

134 - Friday, August 18, 2006

Verrrry Interesting ...
**Professional Hypnotism Manual:
A Practical Approach for Modern Times**
by John G. Kappas, Ph.D.

136 - Sunday, August 20, 2006

More straight talk ...
**How to Talk to a Liberal (If You Must):
The World According to Ann Coulter**
by Ann Coulter

138 - Friday, August 25, 2006

Whiiiiiiine ... now I want a VACATION!
Tikal: A Handbook of the Ancient Maya Ruins
by William R. Coe

140 - Friday, September 15, 2006

Most recent book finished ...
**A Forest of Kings:
The Untold Story of the Ancient Maya**
by Linda Schele & David Freidel

142 - Tuesday, September 26, 2006

Finally ...
The Commanding Self
by Idries Shah

144 - Thursday, September 28, 2006

Skipping ahead again ...
The Prophet Returns
by Gunther Schaule

146 - Saturday, September 30, 2006

Catching up ...
What Survives?: Contemporary Explorations of Life After Death
by Gary Doore, Ed.

147 - Thursday, October 5, 2006

Hyperspace ...
Hyperspace: A Scientific Odyssey through Parallel Universes, Time Warps, and the Tenth Dimension
by Michio Kaku

149 - Saturday, October 14, 2006

Castaneda ...
The Power of Silence: Further Lessons of Don Juan
by Carlos Castaneda

150 - Monday, October 16, 2006

Wish there were more books like this ...
The Teachings of Don Carlos: Practical Applications of the Works of Carlos Castaneda
by Victor Sanchez

151 - Monday, October 30, 2006

Wow ...
An Unlikely Prophet: A Metaphysical Memoir by the Legendary Writer of Superman and Batman
by Alvin Schwartz

153 - Saturday, November 4, 2006

Another recent read ...
Flow: The Psychology of Optimal Experience
by Mihaly Csikszentmihalyi

154 - Sunday, November 5, 2006

More shamanic stuff ...
The Eagle's Gift
by Carlos Castaneda

155 - Wednesday, November 15, 2006

Another good one ...
The Fire from Within
by Carlos Castaneda

157 - Friday, November 24, 2006

Catching up ...
The Book of J
by Harold Bloom & David Rosenberg

159 - Sunday, November 26, 2006

An unusually long read ...
The God Particle:
If the Universe Is the Answer, What Is the Question?
by Leon Lederman & Dick Teresi

160 - Tuesday, November 28, 2006

I should have read this 25 years ago ...
The Opening of the Wisdom Eye
by His Holiness the Dalai Lama, Tenzin Gyatso

162 - Tuesday, November 28, 2006

Catching up ...
Tapihritsa: The Condensed Meaning of an Explanation of the Teachings of Yungdrung Bon
by Lopön Tenzin Namdak

163 - Thursday, November 30, 2006

A fabulous read ...
Crazy Wisdom
by Chögyam Trungpa

165 - Friday, December 8, 2006

hmmm ...
The Enlightened Mind: An Anthology of Sacred Prose
by Stephen Mitchell

167 - Sunday, December 10, 2006

an interesting read ...
The Journey from Eden: The Peopling of Our World
by Brian M. Fagan

169 - Monday, December 11, 2006

Very nice ...
The Symbolism of the Tarot:
Philosophy of Occultism in Pictures and Numbers
by P.D. Ouspensky

171 - Wednesday, December 20, 2006

Eh, might as well get this review done too ...
Compassion In Action:
Setting Out on the Path of Service
by Ram Dass & Mirabai Bush

173 - **QR Code Links**

201 - **Contents - Alphabetical By Author**

213 - **Contents - Alphabetical By Title**

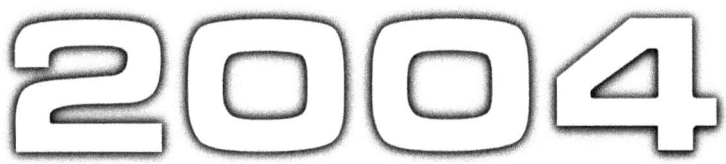

Wednesday, February 4, 2004[1]

books ...

One of the counter-intuitive things about my years of running Eschaton Books was that, in my 14-hour/day 7-day/week schedule I never had time to read anything that wasn't a manuscript submission. Now, I used to read 2-3 books a week back in my P.R. days, and this was always a frustration for me. Well, it took a while, but I'm finally back to reading a bit. I've got a "new system" going, where I have one book running in the middle bathroom, one book in the front bathroom, and one out in the living room ... so that pretty much any non-computer place that I'm likely to *sit* for any length of time has a book handy! I'd had a few books that I'd been "reading" for over a year that I've finally finished up, so I'm now into "all new" (if one can count them as "new", being pulled from a two-deep bookshelf of probably 100+ books that I've bought and not read over the past decade) books.

I just finished Philip Corso's The Day After Roswell[2] (which I bought a week or so back on the strong suggestion of polaris93[3]) today, which was a pretty quick read. Yesterday I *finally* finished Roger Schank's Tell Me A Story[4], which is a fascinating look at memory and intelligence, but something that I've been plowing through for well over a year. So, as of today I have three new books going ... Zen Physics: The Science of Death, the Logic of Reincarnation[5] by David Darling, Treason[6] by the incomparable Ann Coulter, and Breaking the Maya Code[7] by Michael D. Coe ... and I'm already 20% through the first two.

Right now I'm considering a couple of job possibilities which would *not* be "think work" (since I can't seem to find any gigs in my previous modes[8], or in my new training) but would pay well, and be somewhat flexible. If I end up in one of these I suspect that I'll be running through books like crazy again, just to keep my brain active!

Notes:

1. http://btripp-books.livejournal.com/8087.html
2. http://amzn.to/2cA7edw
3. http://polaris93.livejournal.com/
4. http://amzn.to/2cSqS0N
5. http://btripp-books.livejournal.com/7525.html
6. http://btripp-books.livejournal.com/6772.html
7. http://btripp-books.livejournal.com/6193.html
8. http://btripp.info/

Sunday, February 22, 2004

Book ...

I just got done reading a very interesting little book, Zen Physics: The Science of Death, the Logic of Reincarnation[2], by astrophysicist David J. Darling. Frankly, the title is a *bit* misleading, as the book is not really about "reincarnation" per se, and it isn't about a Zen approach to Physics either. Rather, the first half of the book takes a look at death from the standpoint of modern Western science (typified by Physics), and the second half of the book takes a look at consciousness from the standpoint of traditional Eastern metaphysics (typified by Zen).

What was, perhaps, most attractive about this book is that it doesn't come to any firm conclusions, but points at some very interesting possibilities ... the author leaves it up to the reader if they are going to look at the moon, or the finger pointing to the moon.

In terms of biological units operating in a complex niche, the human idea of "self" is perhaps necessary (after all, without a sense of "self" there would be no drive for "self preservation" and without sufficient levels of self preservation there are no beings to be self-conscious!), but the book suggests that the idea of "self" is illusory (and illustrates how this could be so with many psychological and medical cases), and is likely to be something like the particle/wave duality of subatomic physics, one ground of being "localized" by the presence of the "observational equipment" of the human brain ... i.e., we feel "ourself" because there is a brain to "observe" the field of selfhood.

Although he does not specifically cite this in the book, this reminds me of the relation of *Atman* with *Brahman*, the individual self being only a temporary localization of the ultimate beingness (often described as being a drop of sea spray, which is not other than the sea, and which will subsume into the sea once its flight is over).

The second half of the book looks at Eastern thought, and how especially the Mahayana Buddhist thread has approximated the strange complexities of modern physics. He uses Zen as an example (and specifically Rinzai Zen, with its use of Koans to stop the mind and open up moments of pure awareness) of how to reach the reality behind the surface of the observed world.

Anyway, I thought I'd pass this along ... it certainly was well worth the reading!

Notes

1. http://btripp-books.livejournal.com/7525.html

2. http://amzn.to/2cn7xWF

Friday, February 27, 2004[1]

Another book ...

"I know what you're thinking. Did he fire six shots or only five? Well, to tell you the truth, in all this excitement, I've kind of lost track myself. But being as this is a .44 Magnum - the most powerful handgun in the world, and would blow your head clean off, you've got to ask yourself one question: Do I feel lucky? Well, do ya punk?"

Oh, yeah ... the quote, nothing to do with Pooh, of course ... that's Dirty Harry[2] ... But *in all the excitement* I almost forgot to mention finishing up another book. Hmm ... I wonder if there could be a *Tao of Harry Callahan*? Maybe not.

Anyway, I just got done with The Tao of Pooh[3] last night, not being a particularly monumental accomplishment, in that it's only a hundred fifty pages or so. What to say about it? Well, it was very hard keeping it (and the follow-up, The Te of Piglet[4]) in one place, as The Girls kept wandering off with them, thinking that they were books for *them*. Of course, I would not *mind* having The Girls become conversant with Taoist principles at their young ages, but I think the book is still a bit dense for an 8-year-old, let alone the 4-year-old. I, of course, have read much Taoism in the past *{dusts off the B.A. in Religion}* so the *concepts* being presented were not new, and using Pooh and Co. as a basis for teaching stories on that material seem fairly natural. If one had NO exposure to Taoism, this would probably be a very accessible first step.

I have one odd caveat, however. Now, as a lad, I did read the *original* Winnie The Pooh books, but my memories of these must have been subsequently filtered through the Disney Pooh, as I hardly recognized the characters at all. There was a "harder edge" to the original characterizations (such as Eeyore being quite caustic rather than just gloomy) which sort of shocks in this (as the original Pooh books are the source material here). I hadn't recalled that when Kanga and Roo showed up in the 100-Acre Woods they were seen as some monstrous threat that needed to be done away with ... Imagine *that* in the Disney cartoon version! Anyway, I'd say this was a nice way to introduce Taoism to a Western audience.

Oh, another thing almost lost "in all this excitement" ... I wrote *a poem* yesterday! Now, I hadn't written anything since last fall, and with all the change that has come crashing down on me, you might think there would be a thematic, or at least a tonal, shift, *n'est-ce pas?* Well, *mais, non!* ... it was undifferentiable from my prior scribblings, six month, a year, three years back. Sigh. Of course, one of these days I'll transcribe this (and those from last fall and those from the notebook prior which has not been dealt with), and foist these dour musings on all and sundry. Lucky you.

Notes:
1. http://btripp-books.livejournal.com/7337.html
2. https://goo.gl/riNeUK
3. http://amzn.to/2cn5IZR
4. http://btripp-books.livejournal.com/7086.html

Friday, March 5, 2004[1]

another book ...

One has to wonder *what happened* to Benjamin Hoff in the 10 years between his two Pooh/Tao books ... Where *The Tao of Pooh*[2] was charming, disarmingly naive, and well grounded in Taoist text, *The Te of Piglet*[3] is abrasive, confrontational, even petulant! Despite starting off by bragging how well *The Tao of Pooh*[4] did, how many languages it was translated into, etc., etc., etc., Hoff then launches into a series of attacks at "types" he identifies with various Pooh characters. You get the feeling that he feels slighted by certain sorts of people, and he's decided to write a new book to simply get revenge. He takes Rabbit, Tigger, Eeyore, and Owl and uses them as symbols for various people (or behavior patterns) that he clearly *doesn't like*. It would be one thing if he really based any of this on the Taoist texts, but he seems to interject these quotes randomly to very little illustrative effect.

About half way through the book he gives up savaging his character-represented targets and launches into a wider *political* diatribe. Suddenly neither the Pooh world nor the Taoist teachings mean anything, it's all "raging against the machine" at this point. It is almost as though he went out to see "Roger & Me" (released in 1989, while *Piglet* came out in 1992) and suddenly deeply wanted to be Michael Moore, complete with the "selective editing", ignoring of facts, and attacks substituting for truth.

His premise for advocating for the "Piglet" type of approach reads more like a farce of Jimmy Carter's pitiful M.E.O.W. policy (the "Moral Equivalent Of War") than anything from the Taoist material. Where he talks of Charles Dickens being *"... wary of social reformers as they tended to turn people away from the causes they so seriously championed, thereby unwittingly weakening their own efforts"*, a few pages prior he is railing like an A.N.S.W.E.R.[5] stooge about how *"For years now, intelligent, concerned activists have been Out, and self-centered ignoramus conservatives have been In."* ... and he hits on nearly *every* "hot button" of the far-left. Frankly, a better title of this book would be *"The Green Party Piglet Manifesto"*.

Ultimately, *The Te of Piglet*[6] reminds me of the board games made to play off the popularity of mid-70's TV programs ... they all were disappointing as they ended up being yet another version of Parcheesi, with new graphics. Hoff tries to play off the popularity of *Pooh* with a fraudulent follow-up which is neither *about* the Pooh world nor Taoism, but uses the imagery of both simply to pretty up what would be an otherwise unreadable mish-mash of personal vendetta and delusional political rant.

Of course, some of my more Liberal readers might find it quite to their liking.

Notes:
1. http://btripp-books.livejournal.com/7086.html
2. http://btripp-books.livejournal.com/7337.html
3. http://amzn.to/2cUKvsc
4. http://btripp-books.livejournal.com/7337.html
5. http://www.wnd.com/2002/11/15779/
6. http://amzn.to/2cUKvsc

Tuesday, March 9, 2004[1]

more books ...

Well, I've *already* had flak from my Liberal readers over this one ... but it is a GREAT READ, especially if you self-identify as a conservative. If you're a Liberal and wonder why people like me *loathe* the Clintons, spit when Jimmy Carter gets mentioned, and make puking noises when *The New York Times* or the big-3 Network News organizations are cited as "unbiased" sources, Ann Coulter's Treason: Liberal Treachery from the Cold War to the War on Terrorism[2] would go a long way towards enlightening you ... although I doubt most self-identifying Liberals would be able to read this through. To be honest, Ann's tone throughout this book *is* on the caustic side (I was frequently reminded of an old SNL skit where William F. Buckley was depicted debating a small black girl on some obscure historic topic, and ruthlessly taunting her total lack of knowledge of the subject and subsequent tears), which I could have done without, but the subject matter is BRUTALLY HONEST regarding the seditious nature of the Liberal movement (and Democratic Party) over the past century.

Thematically, this is actually *two* books, as the first half looks at the Left's assault on Joe McCarthy, and the second half follows what became a pattern of Leftist attack under the scream *"McCarthyism!"* ever since. I was AMAZED to find that virtually everything I "knew" about Joe McCarthy was a deliberate Leftist spin, spread by the media. 90% of what I would have said was "McCarthyism" were I asked to define it had NOTHING TO DO with Senator McCarthy, but *everything* to do with the campaign of lies, slander, and intentional deception directed against him. Ann takes apart the Liberal smear campaign on McCarthy, looks case-by-case at what he uncovered in light of the fairly recent de-classification of Soviet espionage files, and shows how the truth was systematically distorted by the media and the "liberal elite". It is a sickening story of Traitors in high places. Too bad the story did not stop with the post-war period, but the pattern had been set ... the Left had a "big win" against McCarthy and now had a brush with which to paint *any* non-Leftist figure. The rest of the book shows how this played out through Vietnam, the end of the Cold War, and into the vile Carter and Clinton administrations. I frankly wish that *every* American would read this book, as it throws a harsh spotlight onto the "vast Left-wing conspiracy" which has sought unceasingly to destroy America.

So, what should I follow-up Treason[3] with? Why, wouldn't Ann's Slander: Liberal Lies About the American Right[4] be a natural? Sure it would! This has slotted into Reading Zone #1, while Reading Zone #2 has (replacing *The Te of Piglet*[5]) the fascinating book on Native American spirituality (and politics) God Is Red[6]. I'm still plowing through Breaking the Maya Code[7] in Reading Zone #3, but given the comparable lengths, and "ease of reading", I expect to have new books running in #1 and #2 before moving on to something fresh in #3 (being that Reading Zone #3 is the Big Comfy Chair in the living room, there is always the sleep/read conflict to deal with there as well).

Notes:

1. http://btripp-books.livejournal.com/6772.html
2-3. http://amzn.to/2cn3gCE
4. http://btripp-books.livejournal.com/6510.html
5. http://btripp-books.livejournal.com/7086.html
6. http://btripp-books.livejournal.com/5520.html
7. http://btripp-books.livejournal.com/6193.html

Monday, March 15, 2004[1]

Buy this book! BUY THIS BOOK!

OK ... so as noted here not too many days back, I really liked Ann Coulter's Treason[2], even though it did have a bit of a "pit bull" edge on it. Well, Slander: Liberal Lies About the American Right[3] is even MORE fun, largely because Ann is a bit less in "attack mode" in this one. Whereas Treason[4] looks at the seditious acts of the Left in general and the Democratic Party in particular (odd how every time there's a treasonous scum in the news, there's a raft of Democrats making excuses for their treachery!), Slander[5] takes a look at how the Media treats conservatives and Republicans.

I think my favorite part of this book is how Ann gleefully rattles off the results of Lexis/Nexis searches ... while the Leftist press is claiming to be "middle of the road", their tracks are anything but ... with 10/1 or worse preponderance of "biased to the left" stories or negative mentions of conservatives/Republicans.

I wish Ann had done some charts of all this. It becomes obvious that if the political spectrum were line-graphed from 1 to 9, with 1 being blood-soaked Stalinist Lefties, and 9 being skin-head neo-Nazis, and the actual "middle of the road" being at 5, then what the Liberal Media sees "a centrist stand" is somewhere about *3*! Anything from 4 on up is viewed as "conservative", so even a Left-Centrist Republican can, in the Media's universe, be held up as a "conservative voice". The book has TONS of references (the notes, were they in as large a font as the body of the book, would probably be another third as long), and it has got to irk the Dan Rathers of this world to have *their own words* used to show them for the Leftist Scum that they are!

Of course, my *least* favorite part of the book was the last chapter when Ann goes to the defense of the "Religious Right", although to her credit, she did make it seem less "monolithic" than my preconceptions of it. Why can't Conservatives like Ann (and the WND crew) "do conservatism" without bringing in Christianity? Christianity is as much a delusional scam as the Leftist/Liberal political doctrine. These folks have *seriously* got to read more Ayn Rand and less New Testament!

Anyway, this is another book that I wish EVERYBODY would read. Heck, you can get it new/used from Amazon for under $4 ... what's holding you back?

I decided to shift something "lighter" into my reading spot being vacated by Slander[6], so I'm about to launch into P.J. O'Rourke's All The Trouble In The World[7] which appears to be a bit of a travelogue of all the nasty places he had to visit whilst writing for *Rolling Stone*.

Notes:
1. http://btripp-books.livejournal.com/6510.html
2. http://btripp-books.livejournal.com/6772.html
3. http://amzn.to/2caJbQ6
4. http://btripp-books.livejournal.com/6772.html
5-6. http://amzn.to/2caJbQ6
7. http://btripp-books.livejournal.com/5799.html

Friday, March 19, 2004[1]

Another book ...

Well, I have finally finished plowing through this one. Not that it was a *tedious* read, but it involved a bit more focus than some of the other things I've been reading. Having been a big fan of Mayan archaeology my whole adult life, I found the subject of this more interesting than most folks would have. What I found *fascinating* was that the Mayan glyphs were not properly translated until just the past few decades ... my first trip to the Yucatan was in the late 70's, and that was just when all this stuff started falling into place. Hmmm ... maybe that's why the rates at the *Villas Archaeologicas* started to skyrocket soon after!

It was interesting, although off-putting, to read the in-fighting that went on amid the Mayanist crowd over the past century, with cut-throat positioning so that certain "leading lights" could have their own pet theories stand un-challenged. Interesting that it was a Russian linguist who came up with the key to the decipherment, although having never visited the ruins! The book ends, frankly, with this sort of up in the air, as there seems to be a deep divide between the "dirt archaeologists" and the folks doing the analysis, with the former pretty much ignoring the advances of the latter. Despite the in-fighting in the field, it does make me wonder where I would have ended up were I to have followed a path that seemed open to me in my freshman year at Northwestern ... the folks in the Religion department there were offering me the possibility of doing my Masters concurrently with my B.A., making the classes for the former my electives for the latter, and graduating with both degrees simultaneously (I rather wowed them with my research papers when taking junior/senior level courses in my first year) ... and the probably moving on to the Oriental Institute. Oh, well ... it's a long story why that did not play out that way, best held for some more mopey time. The gist of this being that I would have been hitting the Anthropological/Archaeological world right around the time the Mayan stuff was falling into place.

All in all, Breaking the Maya Code[2] is a worthwhile read if one has any interest in Mayan stuff. Of course, there is a shadow over all this ... now that we *can* read Mayan writing, it only serves to highlight the painful fact that there is *so little left* of the Mayan heritage to read! Coe touches on this in one of the later chapters ... all there remains of a wide, cohesive culture (in that the myths, symbols, etc., were common to many different "culture groups" and across warring political and dynastic borders), are the stone carvings of the ruins, three or four codexes, and pottery shards. The Christians took care of all the rest, burning every scrap of writing (and the Mayans had many, many books, along with the inscriptions on everyday items) they could lay their hands on, because the glyphic writing "looked demonic" ... and the Conquistadors' records talk of vast bonfires of these irreplaceable texts. I can not understand how anybody of good will can tolerate that religion ... it's history is nothing but oppression, bloodshed, and enforced ignorance!

Anyway, as I've noted, I have a good decade's worth of books that I bought but never got around to reading while I was running Eschaton ... and, unfortunately, a lot of the stuff that's stacked up here is a bit on the old side ... at least in terms of books that were written as "cutting edge science", putting in a decade on the shelf might lead to "stale content". I'm hoping that's not the case with the next book, The Light at the Edge of the Universe[3] which is sub-titled *"Leading Cosmologists on the Brink of a Scientific Revolution"*. Ten years is a long time to be hanging "on the brink" of a "revolution", so I hope I'm not going through this whole thing saying "yeah, yeah, I read about that *ages* ago"!

Notes:

1. http://btripp-books.livejournal.com/6193.html
2. http://amzn.to/2calEhd
3. http://btripp-books.livejournal.com/5972.html

Saturday, March 27, 2004[1]

Another book ...

Well, I knew gong in on this that a lot of it might sound like "old news", as what might have been *"Leading Cosmologists on the Brink of a Scientific Revolution"* (as per the sub-title) 10 years or so back, might be less pressing or impressive these days. Of course, as I'd not been particularly "keeping up" over the past decade on advances in the cosmology field, much of the deep-space research and cold dark matter theory was new to me, but it *was* irritating to hear griping about the Hubble (as this was published before NASA fixed it), given its impressive production in recent years.

The Light at the Edge of the Universe[2] is something of an odd book. It was written by Michael Lemonick, a science writer for the likes of *TIME*, rather than a researcher, and frequently reminds one of a travel program as the author goes visiting various astrophysicists around the US. It is filled with strange details (Lemonick seems to insist of painting an unflattering word picture of each of the scientists he talks to ... what point is there if Dr. X looks "rumpled" or Dr. Y has a receding hairline, especially if you're including photos of each?) which have little bearing on the point of the narrative. Of course, there is no "point", really, as it a survey of different people's work on inter-related scientific issues ... I only wish it didn't have quite the "what I did on my summer vacation" feel to it. Oh, well.

I have another half dozen or so books on similar topics (cosmology, etc.) waiting for me, but I felt I needed to disengage from this a bit to be able to go into the next "serious" book fresh, so I'm taking a bit of a break for the middle reading station and jumping into William Gibson's now-classic Neuromancer[3], which has likewise been sitting on the shelf for the past decade (but I trust that this will have "aged better" than the early 90's "cutting edge science" things!).

Notes:

http://btripp-books.livejournal.com/5972.html

http://amzn.to/2caGDla

http://btripp-books.livejournal.com/5344.html

Tuesday, April 6, 2004[1]

Cool book!

O.K. ... this did not come off my shelf, but was in a stack of books from my Mom's place. Among the myriad of ways that I'm going to be missing my Mother is that she'd buy a lot of conservative books and pass them along to me when she was done, so I sort of figured I'd slip this in for my recent "political/philosophical" book slot. P.J. O'Rourke's All The Trouble In The World[2] is a FUN read ... there have been dozens of quotes I'd have liked to share out of this, but wasn't reading with a highlighter, so you're out of luck (hey ... Amazon has this used for as little as 59¢, so it wouldn't kill ya to pick a copy up!). Once again, this would have probably had more impact 5 years ago (it's 10 years old at this point, so there's a lot of Clinton/Gore poking going on), but it was a hoot.

The main thrust of All The Trouble In The World: The Lighter Side of Overpopulation, Famine, Ecological Disaster, Ethnic Hatred, Plague, and Poverty[3] is O'Rourke musing on "human suffering" in the context of various places he's been around the world ... *over-population* in the context of Bangaladesh (he points out that the population density there is the same as Fremont, CA) ... *famine* in the context of Somalia ... *environment* in the context of the Amazon rain forest ... *ecology* in the context of the Czech Republic ... *saving the earth* in the context of the Earth Summit in Rio ... *multiculturalism* in the context of his alma mater, Miami of Ohio, and the Balkans ... *plague* in the context of Haiti ... And *economic justice* in the context of Vietnam. In almost every case, the core problem is one of *politics* and not environment or economics. In fact, by the time you're half way through this book, you're pretty sure that the old saw about the Klintons *(Q: "How can you tell if the Klintons are lying?" A: "Their lips are moving!")* goes double for every "environmentalist" (and he seems particularly fond of poking Al Gore with sharp sticks). Virtually every statement from the Environmental Left is shown to be blown up from some totally-out-of-context bit of untreated preliminary research which was grabbed to make a hot sound bite (the Alar debacle is a prime example). Section by section he shows what a colossal mess governments make of the world where given the chance ... a Libertarian battle-cry if I've ever heard one. The book ends on a positive note with the grass-roots capitalism erupting from Vietnam ... a situation he says was made possible when *"Faced with a choice of leading or following, the Vietnamese government got out of the way."*.

As I noted above, this is available for under $5 (with shipping) through Amazon's used department ... if you're sick of the smarmy liars like Al Gore spewing shit they've made up to further their political agendas, pick up a copy of this book ... you'll be happy that you did! Anyway, since I had such fun reading this, I dug up another P.J. O'Rourke book from the depths of my "to be read" shelves, Parliament of Whores[4], where he takes a good hard look at *our* government. Should be fun

Notes:
1. http://btripp-books.livejournal.com/5799.html
2-3. http://amzn.to/2cqrA47
4. http://btripp-books.livejournal.com/5063.html

Friday, April 9, 2004[1]

A BRILLIANT BOOK!

This was a truly amazing book ... one that I wish everybody would pick up. Vine Deloria, Jr., an American Indian activist, takes a look at the conflict between "western culture" and "tribal culture" and basically distills the issue down to Christianity. While I am a long-time ardent "anti-Christian", I have rarely seen the case made so calmly, and so directly. The Christian apologists often brush aside folks like me a "still rebelling against their upbringing", as though there was *nothing* within the dominant paradigm which was worth opposing. This is one of the unique points of God Is Red: A Native View of Religion[2], the author stands OUTSIDE of the Christian tradition and is able to dissect its history without the encumbrances of being a part of that. Here are some *sweet* quotes:

> "Where the Cross goes, there is ... only death, destruction, and ultimately betrayal."

> "Average Christians when hearing of the disaster wreaked ... by their religion and its adherents are quick to state, 'But the people who did this were not really Christians.' In point of fact, they really were Christians. In their day they enjoyed all the benefits and prestige that Christendom could confer. They were cheered as heroes of the faith, ... that a Christian society might be build on the ruin of pagan villages."

> "It is interesting to note that [leading researchers] have determined that monotheism was almost always a product of the political arrangement of a society and not the natural product of religious activities or experiences."

> "It is my opinion that popular American Christianity is the greatest of all blasphemies in world history."

Now, not everything in this book was as *agreeable* to me as the author's views on Christianity ... he is somewhat dismissive of Whites like myself who have sought within the Native teachings pathways to the divine. I am, perhaps, closer to understanding the radical Native stance that this is "theft" of their beliefs, but it still seems to me a bit askew, considering that *some* tribes and traditions are explicit in their mythologies of the need to spread their knowledge to the other races. Deloria favors the re-establishment of "homeland" faiths for those of us of European stock, noting the Druidic and Nordic faiths reappearing despite millennia of Christian suppression (although he also cautions on this, given the way the Germanic faith expressed itself in the Nazi movement).

Anyway ... anybody who feels "uncomfortable" with Christianity and can't quite put their finger on the reason why should READ THIS BOOK ... also, anybody who can't understand WHY folks like me *hate* Christianity so deeply should *also* read this book. It is a bright revealing spotlight shining in the dark recesses of Christianity (and Western Culture), tracking the historic bases and failings of the Major Monotheisms (Judaism and Islam also get a once-over, but they weren't the engines for obliteration of the Native American culture the way Christianity was ... although Islam is doing a pretty good imitation of the "destroying Church" these days!). And, heck ... you can get it for as little as $8 though Amazon's "used" (although "like new") links!

I was having a hard time deciding what to slot into the "religion/spirituality" reading niche after this ... I've opted to try to plow through the rather formidable-looking Voices of the First Day[3], which appears to be a look at how Australian aboriginal culture and faith has struggled in *its* conflict with the Western Christian paradigm.

Notes:

1. http://btripp-books.livejournal.com/5520.html
2. http://amzn.to/2cRBOjq
3. http://btripp-books.livejournal.com/1385.html

Tuesday, April 13, 2004[1]

It's a classic ...

Well, I finally got around to reading Neuromancer[2] ... I had the hard-cover "10th Anniversary Edition" sitting around for a long time (it's well past the 20th anniversary now), and just hadn't gotten to it. Needless to say (it hardly needs *my* endorsement), it's a very good read. I found certain aspects of it quite interesting ... primarily the fact that when I nodded off reading it, the book "continued" in my dream states (albeit not as written by Mr. Gibson). Having seen The Matrix (well, the first two movies so far) prior to having read the book, there was a lot of "filtering" going on as I recognized themes and images from the films in their raw state in the book. I now want to read Gibson's other books as well.

I'm afraid that I'm going to become tiresome in my reiteration of this point ... but nearly all my "to be read" shelves' contents have been there for a decade (as I've mentioned before, in the 10 years that I ran Eschaton[3] I worked pretty much 14-hour days, 7 days a week, and if it didn't have something to do with the business, it didn't get done ... so pretty much the *only* stuff I read during that time were manuscripts!). This leads me into situations, especially in the "cutting edge science" category (1/3 of my reading) of getting "old news". I'm afraid that this is going to again be the case with the next book in that slot, The Edges of Science[4] by Richard Morris, which is *so old* (it came out in 1990) that neither Amazon nor B&N have a cover image ... on the plus side, though, if I end up really liking it, I can recommend the Amazon used link, which has it for as little as little as 75 cents! *{edit: While Googling around looking for a cover image, I discovered that this is on the Church of All World's "Bibliography" page ... which makes me think I may find it of more interest than I was anticipating!}*

Notes:

1. http://btripp-books.livejournal.com/5344.html
2. http://amzn.to/2camnjv
3. http://www.eschatonbooks.com/
4. http://btripp-books.livejournal.com/4759.html

Thursday, April 22, 2004[1]

Another good book!

Well, finished this other P.J. O'Rourke book ... in which he takes a long hard look at American government. As you would expect, it's another fun read ... from his section headings (such as "The Three Branches of Government: Money, Television, And Bullshit" and "Our Government: What The Fuck Do They Do All Day And Why Does It Cost So Goddamn Much Money?") to his *hilarious* classification of the "Perennially Indignant" (you know, those types that form the reliable mass of any demonstration). Even though the book was written in the early days of the first Bush administration (the initial sections of the book are about the election process, with on-the-scenes reports from the '88 election cycle which sound almost *historical* at this point), but the points O'Rourke makes are still current. Most of what the government does could be done far more effectively (you should see him "solve" the budget!), and most of the folks who want the government to "DO SOMETHING" rarely want the government to FIX their pet issues, just throw money at it (and them). In case after case, he shows how the bureaucracy and special interest groups suck up the tax dollars while rarely, if ever, solving any of the problems (most of which would be easily solved by directly approaches like school vouchers).

Parliament of Whores: A Lone Humorist Attempts to Explain the Entire U.S. Government[2] looks at how we elect our government, how the various parts of government function (or not), how various policy areas are formulated and shaped, and how various entrenched interest groups operate. O'Rourke walks the corridors of assorted government agencies and interviews the folks responsible for spending our money. He looks at the wide range of what our government does, from the gross inefficiencies of our near-Stalinist farm policies to the efficiency and surprising economy of our military establishment. And, hey, as I mentioned before, it's a cheap read if you get it used from Amazon!

Staying somewhat "within genre", the next book moving into my politics/society reading slot is Hunter S. Thompson's Songs of the Doomed[3]. I have been a "fan at a distance" of HST for years, more for his image than having read much of his stuff. I have some trepidation of coming in on "vol 3" of the Gonzo Papers, but I'm guessing that Thompson's writing is not based on a whole heck of a lot of linearity which would require me to have handy recall of the first two books in this grouping! Once again, like Parliament of Whores[4], this may suffer a bit in topicality from "shelf burn", but I'm trusting that HST will have enough biting wit in his observations that they will still find bone fourteen years after their writing.

Notes:
1. http://btripp-books.livejournal.com/5063.html
2. http://amzn.to/2cfLkwZ
3. http://btripp-books.livejournal.com/4222.html
4. http://amzn.to/2cfLkwZ

Wednesday, May 5, 2004[1]

another book ...

What a pain in the ass .. I am discovering that I'm having to *scan* these covers in at this point, since the books I'm getting to are SO old (in web terms) that neither Amazon nor B&N have the graphics for me to grab! Lazy slob that I am, this is putting a major crimp in my enthusiasm for maintaining the "format" of these little reviews here. I guess on the good side (from *your* standpoint) is that some of these are going for WAY cheap in the "used" departments ... heck, you can get the current title here for as little as 50¢ though Amazon's used service ... such a deal!

Anyway, in this book Richard Morris takes the reader from the basics of physics and into progressively more speculative areas of cosmology. Again, this came out in 1990, so a lot of what was "new theory" then has been hashed over quite a bit in the intervening years, this seems especially true for stuff like the various "string" theories. I actually had a practical use of the info here, as one of the crossword answers in the American in-flight magazine on the trip out to Boston was "lepton", and I'd read the particle part of this recently enough to be able to come up with that pretty much off the top of my head!

I'd taken this on the road with me largely due to it being the smallest (HxW) of the books I'm currently reading. I was also having a hard time *reading* this ... while the material was interesting, I found myself *falling asleep* with much more frequency while reading The Edges of Science: Crossing the Boundary from Physics to Metaphysics[2] than is typically the case. I guess this is a indictment of the writing, although it was not a "chore", I had a hard time keeping awake while working my way through it (for example, I'd taken it along to fill time during Daughter #2's ballet class today and dropped it on the floor *three times* during her hour class!). Again, if one was not overly familiar with modern physics/cosmology, this book would be a good walk-through of a lot of the major areas, going from the "hard science" bits and out to the "metaphysical" stuff. It has a particularly nice glossary in the back, which gives decent thumbnails definitions of most of the major terms, which is a helpful thing when one starts getting hazy on the difference between Cosmic Strings and Superstring, let alone "Balls of Wall"!

At the end of The Edges of Science[3] it covers the "anthropic principle" (and I'm a believer in the "weak anthropic" version ... which says the universe that we see is the way it is because if it *wasn't* that way, there would be no sentient beings to *see* it ... with the implication that there are or have been countless *other* universes with varying properties), this takes center stage in the next book going into my "science" reading slot, Cosmic Coincidences[4] by John Gribbin and Martin Rees. It was a toss-up between that and another book which was taking a *philosophical* view on the same subjects, and I frankly went with this one because the other had little bitty cramped type, and I didn't feel quite like torturing myself that way at the moment (that's another good deal ... what cost me $20 for the hardcover in 1989 is now available in paperback for under a buck used at Amazon)!

Notes:

1. http://btripp-books.livejournal.com/4759.html
2-3. http://amzn.to/2cal3NB
4. http://btripp-books.livejournal.com/4534.html

Thursday, May 20, 2004[1]

Another book down ...

Bah ... another cover I had to scan! I'm too lazy for this shit!

Anyway ... yep, somehow knocked down the physics book before the others (well, that Aboriginal Culture book I'm reading is going to take *forever* at the rate it's going and the size it is ... I was afraid of that when I slotted it!). Cosmic Coincidences: Dark Matter, Mankind, and Anthropic Cosmology[2] by John Gribbin and Martin Rees was pretty much what I expected, a walk through the bits of info that lead one to the Anthropic principle. I've read a good deal along these lines over the years, and while I'm in "the weak Anthropic camp", I really can't say which scenario is my bet for the "nature of the universe", as the "multiple universes", "branching universes" and "sequential universes" models all have something to say for themselves. At base, though, it's pretty clear that the *reason* that the universe looks "tailored" to sentient organic life is because we find ourselves existing IN a universe that just happens to have the balance of forces, etc., which could allow for sentient organic life to occur. If the numbers weren't just right, we wouldn't be here to worry about it, and whatever meta-universe model you choose to believe in, that's pretty much the deal.

As I've mentioned *ad nauseam* in here in reference to these physics books ... they're "old" at this point (this one hit the shelf here in 1989), and I'd be quite interested to see what might have *changed* in the 15 years since this was written (once again, this talks about the Hubble telescope as something that is yet to happen). There were some very useful technical explanations in here that I hadn't hit previously, details on space curvature, cosmic string geometry, etc., which was good to get. I think the book ended weakly, however, as their actual *discussion* of the various degrees (or not) of Anthropic cosmological thought was far less definitive than the science preceding it. Once again, though, the age of the book makes it quite a deal, as Amazon has used copies of this for *under a buck*!

Since I was left "hungry" at the end of this, I decided to slip in Universes[3] by John Leslie (not the porn star[4] of that name, I trust!) next in my "science" slot. This is a "philosophy" book specifically dealing with the questions of Anthropic thought, and actually uses the "G" word (obviously, the folks who hold that God created the whole huge universe just to serve as a backdrop for regional human theatrics, have an *extreme* form of Anthropism kicking around their befuddled heads) ... so I have *some* trepidation that this will be navel-gazing via Oxford and not so much a "scientific discussion" of the topic (although I will admit, the concept of God as "creative tinkerer" has a certain appeal ... imagine the Deity setting up parameters for a universe and then "setting it off" like a kid with an M80 just to see what flies off where!).

I don't know what I'm going to do when I finish that H.S.T. book ... I don't have anything particularly "political/sociological" that I feel like slogging through at the moment. I hate to think of going out and *buying* a book for that (given that I have many dozens of unread books sitting around waiting for me to get to them), but somehow I just can't "pull the trigger" on the few titles on hand which would fit. Perhaps (since that Australian book is going to take forever), I could slide a few "religion/spirituality" books through there until I find something appropriate.

Yeah, like you care what I'm reading ... hah!

Notes:

1. http://btripp-books.livejournal.com/4534.html
2. http://amzn.to/2cfFETM
3. http://btripp-books.livejournal.com/2919.html
4. https://en.wikipedia.org/wiki/John_Leslie_(director)

Monday, May 24, 2004[1]

Bad Craziness ...

So, I was getting this post pulled together, and all of a sudden my computer re-booted ... coincidence, or *conspiracy*?

My brain can't handle much more bad craziness, but that's what Dr. Thompson specializes in ... and after having to deal with two separate Temples of Mammon today, I'm almost ready to storm the gates, the only problem being my pointed lack of the necessary drugs, booze, cash, weapons, and high-powered vehicles. Damn. I guess my own insanity will have to wait for another day. As it was, I had to go back and re-construct all the links and stuff for this, which is making me cranky, on top of being in a deep pit of neurosis brought on by this afternoon's errands. Sucks to be me, I guess.

I don't think it necessarily sucks to be Dr. Hunter S. Thompson, since he would appear to be rarely "there", only present as the animating spirit of his drug/booze/adrenaline soaked body, and the piquant literary filter by which those over-the-edge experiences reach the page. In Songs of the Doomed : More Notes on the Death of the American Dream[2] he takes us on a rambling journey through the 50's, 60's, 70's and 80's, flashing in and out of memories/stories with little connection or coherence, yet as a whole, they offer a window into his particular brand of insanity, sometimes filed under "Gonzo". One wonders what to make of some of the abrupt story ends, and certainly of the chaotic closure to the book ... again, I have an early version here (1990, the same year as the last entries in it) and the currently available edition[3] might have some of the many extremely loose ends tied up ... or not, I suppose.

As I noted a few posts back, I did not have a "ready" political/social book to slot in to follow this (or at least one that I was up for reading at the moment). So, I took a close look at the "to be read" bookshelves and discovered a title that *should* have certain logical lead-ins from Thompson, Why the Reckless Survive[4] by Melvin Konner, which appears to address the question of what cultural or evolutionary benefits "extreme" behavior might offer for humanity. This is another that I hope I'll be enthused about, as it can be had for under a buck via Amazon's used listings!

Notes:

1. http://btripp-books.livejournal.com/4222.html
2-3. http://amzn.to/2cjeJ43
4. http://btripp-books.livejournal.com/3842.html

Thursday, September 23, 2004[1]

Another book ...

Wow ... it's been quite a while since I "knocked down" a book ... I got stuck in a couple of "thick" ones (one thick in body, one thick in prose) and have been dragging through those. This, one, however, was a real treat ... fascinating and beautifully written. Why the Reckless Survive: And Other Secrets of Human Nature[2] is a collection of essays by anthropologist Melvin Konner, looking at various "human mysteries" through lenses of numerous primitive, foreign, and historical cultures. I'm surprised at the negative reviews this got, as it was both engrossing and a pleasure to read. Like many of the things I have been finally getting off my to-be-read shelves, this comes from 1990, and it appears to have been long out of print. Lucky for you, should you be interested in checking it out, as Amazon has used copies for as little as 45¢!

I started reading this one back in June, and it's a testament to the chaos of my life since then that I've only just now finished it (especially given the slow going on the other two books I'm in the midst of). I have been frequently tempted to share long passages from this book with my LJ readers as the perceptions of "human nature" in Why the Reckless Survive[3] are real gems, but I figured that Mr. Konner and his publishers would probably prefer me *not* excerpting half his book on-line here, and I reckon that those intrepid souls who have me on their Friends List would just as well not have reams of stuff to read through. I do recommend getting this one, however, especially as cheaply as it can be had on the used market.

I'm not sure what I'm going to start next ... I'm still plowing through John Leslie's Universes[4], which is quite a struggle as I strongly disagree with his "design" stance and he seems to be grasping at *any* half shred of data that might prove a "created universe". I'm hoping to finish that up before slotting in something new.

Notes:

1. http://btripp-books.livejournal.com/3842.html
2-3. http://amzn.to/2cRysJq
4. http://btripp-books.livejournal.com/2919.html

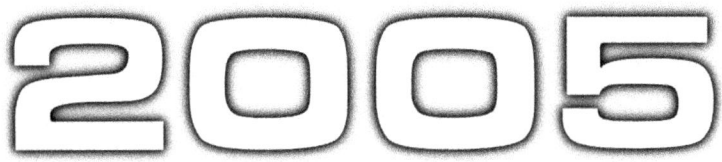

Wednesday, January 5, 2005[1]

Another book ...

So, those of you who have been paying attention know that I've been "stuck" in a couple of books not much to my liking for a few months now, and no doubt recall that I was looking for something to fill time with pool-side while The Girls went swimming last week. Well, The Wife had given me this book as part of my Xmas haul, and I'd already gotten a few chapters into it, so I figured I could do worse. Fork It Over : The Intrepid Adventures of a Professional Eater[2] by restaurant reviewer Alan Richman is not exactly my "standard" reading, but it does hark back to my many years in the food industry and associations with many in the restaurant field (indeed, Mr. Richman and I do have quite a number of common acquaintances), and it did prove itself to be a fun and fast read.

It has been suggested to me a number of times over the past 30 years that I should consider doing food writing ... as I have a reasonably respectable grasp on both food *and* writing ... but I think my "vibe" on that line of work was much like Richman writes about here, a good way to take the joy out of the dining experience! As I was working my way through this book, I was feeling that it didn't "hang together" particularly well, until I realized that this was collection of various pieces written by Richman for *GQ*, *Bon Appetite*, and *Food & Wine* with one or two bits thrown in for continuity. I guess the point of this book is to give "outsiders" a look into the life of a "professional eater", but this, unfortunately, led more to kvetching than to culinary voyeurism.

Sadly, there *were* gems of said "culinary voyeurism" (especially the chapter on truffles), and I found myself reaching for the phone to read passages to my Mom. I worked for my Mother for nearly 20 years doing food P.R., and, naturally enough, my whole "food perception" is tied up with her. Of course, my Mom died just about a year ago (it will a full year in a week), so there's that "slap of reality" every time I, out of habit, want to call her about something. (sigh) I should write a book about the pitfalls of working most of one's adult life with one's parents ... I don't think most folks appreciate what a huge hole their passing leaves for those who are not *just* losing a parent, but a boss, mentor, friend, dining/travel companion, etc. etc. etc.

Notes:

1. http://btripp-books.livejournal.com/3702.html
2. http://amzn.to/2czO4lq

Monday, January 10, 2005[1]

oh, lookie ... another book!

Now, I wouldn't specifically say that I've *abandoned* the books that I've been "stuck in" for the past several months, but I've decided to run some other titles through until such time as I feel like really "fighting" with a couple of books (and those two I've mentioned are *doozies*). So, I jumped into that "foodie" book from Xmas last week, and then more-or-less grabbed a book at random of the "to be read" bookcase. What I ended up with was The Lost Ship of Noah: In Search of the Ark at Ararat[2] by Charles Berlitz, the grandson of the language course guy.

The #1 compliment I can give this book is that it was a fast read. Berlitz has penned a number of books on "mysteries" and I guess he had an interest in Noah's Ark and so opted to cobble this together. When I went searching for a cover graphic to put in here (I ended up having to scan the dust jacket), I found the interesting situation that this book is apparently highly thought of by *both* Bible Thumpers *and* "Newage" types. The second best thing about this book is that you can get a used copy via Amazon for as little as 47¢ ... so if you have a hankering for this sort of thing, it can be had for cheap!

I don't know if the author went out *looking for something* or not ... the book is primarily a "history" of efforts to find the Ark on Mt. Ararat over the past several centuries, with "cloak & dagger" stuff (every reported photo of a wooden ark has mysteriously disappeared along with their owners), and enough "earth changes" pseudoscience that would make Dick Hoagland ill. By the end he's led us to *various* "Arks" up on the mountain (ones melting out of glaciers, ones tuned into stone, etc., etc., etc.) and has turned that into evidence (along with the many cultures with Ark/Flood legends, and many places where ships have been found in mines or on mountains) of world-wide cataclysms (although he does touch on the unlikelihood of enough water being moved around to have many ships run aground at 17,000 feet up a mountain!).

As I've noted previously, most of my book backlog dates to pre-1993, and this one came out in 1987. Now, *some genres* age more gracefully than others, but "the sky is falling!" books tend to have a very short run before they become ridiculous. Unfortunately, towards the end of this book, Berlitz lays on the "prophesies of doom" stuff thick and heavy, with various "end dates" looming ... like 1999, 2000, and 2001 ... as well as agonizing over an "immanent" nuclear war between the US and the USSR (this was a couple of years before the Berlin Wall fell). From the standpoint of 2005, I wonder if I managed to somehow miss the memo regarding the world ending!

Notes:

1. http://btripp-books.livejournal.com/3580.html

2. http://amzn.to/2cfHsrG

Thursday, March 24, 2005[1]

Woot ... finally finished one of these books!

As anybody who's been paying *way too much attention* would have noticed, I haven't put up a "book review" here in quite a while. This is, of course, due to a mix of things, being busy with the business, being busy with the family, and, frankly, being *stuck* in a couple of books that are like dental surgery to read. The current "done" book is not one of those, but one that I, in desperation, yanked off the shelf to have *something* to read at one point when I just *couldn't* face either of the other two in which I'm enmired!

This one, The Essential Kabbalah : The Heart of Jewish Mysticism[2] by Daniel C. Matt, is a scholarly introduction to the Kabbalah. It is not in-depth, nor overly broad, but introduces the reader to many of the classic authors, presenting key excerpts from their work in the "themed" sections, with attributional and explanatory notes in the back.

To be honest, I was worried for a while that this, too, would be another grinding read, as the initial sections on the Sefirot and their alignment on the *Otz Chiim* "Tree of Life" seemed muddied with a level of "poetic mysticism" that I had not previous had to deal with, having the bulk of my experience of the Sefirot coming through the rather idiosyncratic filter of Crowley, and his interpreters. Fortunately, the book moved on from there and became more familiar, if in its echoes of Sufi teachings (which I've read quite a bit of).

Anyway, this would appear to be a pretty good "sampler" of what is involved in Kabbalistic study, and is based on actual *traditional* materials, and not their later pop/new-age permutations! Once again, thanks to Amazon's "new&used" service, you can get a copy of this for as little as $3.25 ... so if The Essential Kabbalah[3] sounds like something you want to check out, you're in luck!

I'm bringing along John Leslie's (no, not *that* John Leslie!) book "Universes" with me this weekend, and I'm hoping that I'll be able to force myself to finally plow through the remainder of it. As I've noted before, I keep wanting to bitchslap the author for his heavy "designist" stance ... of course, this is due to my suspicions that deep inside every "anti-anthropic" theorist there's a scared child not wanting to let go of his or her Sunday school fairy tales ... and my worry that every "Sunday school fairy tale believer" has a strong potential for turning into a jackbooted theocratic thug if their particular fairy tales are threatened! Oh, well ... at least it's easier to force down than the brain curdling newage twaddle of "Voices of the First Day" (the *other* book I've been trying to get through)!

Notes:

1. http://btripp-books.livejournal.com/3231.html
2-3. http://amzn.to/2cfFHLk

Monday, April 4, 2005[1]

Finally ...

OK ... so I *finally* have knocked down one of the two books in which I've been enmired for *months*. I guess I should have read the Amazon customer reviews, as a lot of my complaints about this book were well described there (especially the one titled "Get the bias out of your math!"). As another reviewer noted, the "logic" of the book was very hard to follow, and it was oddly structured with numbered reference points seemingly randomly sprinkled through the text, though this might be due to the author following some academic "philosophy template" which calls for things to be broken up like that, but if you're used to reading *scientific* books on the subject, it borders on gobbledygook (plus he kept using the most *inane* stories/analogies to frame things and *then* constantly referred back to these like he'd established some great touchstone of truth!).

Anyway, John Leslie's Universes[2] purports to take a look at cosmological theories from a philosophical standpoint, primarily bashing together the "designist" and "anthropic" stands on the question of "why is there life here" until the reader's head bleeds. As I pointed out above, there is some question to the veracity of the math used to tear apart the Anthropic side ... the author plainly prefers the scenario of a Deity "making" one universe specifically "designed" to contain life to the possibility of multiple universes (whether isolated or sequential) where life might or might not arise out of the particular mix of states expressed in any particular universe.

I found it interesting that by the end of the book, the author was sort of "backpedaling" from a "hard Deistic" design stance, taking refuge in a "Neo-Platonist" God which was a force of "ethical necessity" ... which if you watered it down much more could just as easily be a pan-theistic "Life Force" with, of course, no means of defining of explaining it. Now, being that I'm on the "weak anthropic" side of things, I don't have any problem with the concept that there might be some sort of "Life Force" that we have yet to find a way to scientifically dissect, so by the end of the book I felt less like I was reading something by a raving Fundy loon, but it was a long hard read without much payoff beyond being DONE with it. Needless to say, I wouldn't recommend rushing out to pick up this one!

Notes:

1. http://btripp-books.livejournal.com/2919.html
2. http://amzn.to/2c6ubmy

Wednesday, April 6, 2005[1]

Well, that sure was different ...

Gee ... as opposed to the last book to appear in this space, it only took me *two days* to blow through Michael Drosnin's Bible Code II: The Countdown[2]! As folks paying attention no doubt recall, I found this at one of the dollar stores a couple of weeks back, and I was sort of interested in getting into it, so once I got *Universes* done, I popped into this. Needless to say, it was a "fast read", primarily due to the many "grids" (see the bottom half of the cover pic) where the "crossword-like" words show up.

I had read the original *Bible Code* book many years ago (maybe eight?), and was interested in seeing the follow-up, given all the brou-ha-ha over the whole theory of the thing (which is, briefly, that the original parts of the Bible, the *Torah*, were delivered to the Hebrews in one long unbroken string of letters, and that a program that looked at any X# of characters might find "hidden codes" in it). While that's all well and good (and it could be argued that one could do something similar with nearly any text string), the essence of the Bible Code theory is in the *groupings* of words and the odds of such groupings being randomly generated. Needless to say, I can't really speak to that aspect of it, but it IS interesting what stuff (the predicted assassination of Rabin, the election of Clinton, the 9/11 attacks) can apparently be coaxed out of it.

Now, many of the books I've been reading have been "staler" than this, but due to the "predictive" nature of the subject, this has gone a bit stale in only a couple of years (published in 2002), as it was expecting a global financial crisis (ala the Great Depression), and was very focused on stuff to do with the late Yasir Arafat. It has, however, *not quite* run out of "the sky is falling" material, as it projects some sort of nuclear attack happening in 2006 (and perhaps a bio/chem attack in 2005), but much of what the author seems to have his panties in a knot about clearly did not play out the way he was expecting.

And, speaking of expectations ... I had *mine* blown away by another aspect of this book. The focus of most of this Bible Code stuff has been prophetic / theological / political, and the biases of the author certainly appear to fall in the latter part of that triad. However, a significant portion of Bible Code II[3] sounds like it comes straight out of the work of Zecharia Sitchin[4]! It seems that, in probing the nature of the code, it gives up clues about buried obelisks, *spaceships*, and even genetic manipulations by *aliens* to engineer modern man! Drosnin spends a not inconsiderable portion of the book chasing down these clues, and even traveling to the Lisan peninsula in the Dead Sea, which is where the code says all this cool super-ancient extraterrestrial stuff should be appearing. How, you ask? Well, the level of the Dead Sea has been dropping about a meter a year, so a lot of what used to be fairly deeply submerged is suddenly above water for the first time in millennia (in this picture[5], everything on the peninsula but for the sharp pointy bit at the very top level was under water as recently as the 60's!).

My biggest complaint about the book (aside from a few bitchy political things) is that it's all a *TEASE* ... he never gets a dig together, never even gets a rough survey done. Of course, he *was* writing during the start of the Intifada, so there was a lot of resistance in Jordan (where Lisan is) to letting a "Jewish expedition" dig on "their" land, but you would think Drosnin could at least leave us with some tantalizing "we found *something*" to lead us into a *Bible Code III*, but he just leaves all that stuff hanging in the midst of the other story lines, which is all *very* frustrating!

Anyway ... what to read *next*? I took a brief count of what's up on my to-be-read shelves and found I have about a gross of books there ... 12 stacks of about 12 books each ... so I have plenty to choose from (as regular readers know, I barely got to read *anything* during the 10 years I was running my own publishing company, thus the huge backlog). I noticed a 3-book set on the mythologies of Central, South, and North America, and am thinking I might plow into those next ... I know, you can *hardly wait* to hear about them!

Notes:

1. http://btripp-books.livejournal.com/2599.html
2-3. http://amzn.to/2c28m9o
4. http://amzn.to/2gZtxHS
5. https://goo.gl/wSQ2TU

Monday, April 11, 2005[1]

Oh, boy ... quick reads are so refreshing!

Yep, knocked down another book in just a few days. I'm nowhere near my pace from back when I was single (and pre-publishing biz), but it's nice to see some "progress"! As I noted at the end of the last book post, I decided to go for a 3-volume set of Native mythology in the Americas, the first volume being North America.

The Mythology of North America[2] is by John Bierhorst, who appears (by all the stuff listed on Amazon) to be a rather prolific author in the genre. I often approach books in the "anthropology" ballpark with some trepidation, as they can be dense and tiresome, this, however (as alluded to in the post's subject) was a "quick read", primarily based on descriptive re-tellings of various myths, along with materials placing the individual myths in their tribal, cultural, and geographical contexts. On this latter point, it was quite interesting seeing the various tribal/cultural groupings mapped out for the various regions. Aside from this, what to say about the book? One either likes reading myths or one doesn't ... I found it entertaining and informative, and was relieved that the presentation was as straight forward as it was.

Once again, if this sounds of interest to you, you're in luck, as the "used" links on Amazon (for the out-of-print hardcover edition) have this going for as little as $1.01 ... such a deal! While I was able to dig up some on-line cover graphics for this (from the paperback edition), I opted to scan the dust jacket of the hardcover, since it was a whole lot cooler looking (which, of course, means I'll have to do this for the other books in the series as well).

Next up (and already sitting out by the "reading chair" in the living room) is Bierhorst's book on South American mythology. Hopefully that will also only take a few days to plow through. Oh, by the way ... I might have a glimmer of hope for getting some traction in that *Voices of the First Day* book that I've been stuck in ... I'm about 17 pages shy of completing "Part One" which seems to be the author's theoretical (gobbledygook) underpinnings, and the subsequent sections seem to be more objective and less delusional ... I still have a couple of hundred pages to get through in that one, but I'm now hoping that the rest of it won't be as painful as the read's been so far!

Notes:

1. http://btripp-books.livejournal.com/2405.html
2. http://amzn.to/2ckD9tK

Sunday, April 24, 2005[1]

Well, that's two out of three ...

Finished up the second installment of the *"Gods and Heroes of the New World"* trilogy (a name that I suspect got tagged onto these books when they went to paperback, as it doesn't appear anywhere in the original hardcover editions, in fact, until the introduction to the *third* book there was no mention that the books were part of a series) by John Bierhorst.

This one is The Mythology of South America[2], which, unsurprisingly, deals with myths, etc. from various native groups in said continent. Like the North American volume that preceded it, this has an interesting structure of being based on regions of inter-related tribal groups (by language, societal structure, etc.), and not standard geographical blocks, which sheds a new light on how some myth structures appear and disappear across a given area.

I found one myth element *fascinating* in this, though ... it was part of a recurring theme in South American myths, of when the Men took over control of society. Now, of course, there is a "truism" in neo-Paganism that at some point in the deep past society was Matriarchic, worshiping a Great Goddess, blah, blah, blah, blah. It is interesting that one set of these myths deals with this, from the *men's* perspective, of how they "threw off the yoke of female oppression" etc. ... but what is most tantalizing here is the blatant admission that *most* of the religious systems and rituals are simply fear/reward matrixes for *maintaining power structures* ... this is the "deep dark secret" of the Men's societies that must never be revealed (under pain of death).

Needless to say, I doubt there is much difference on this level between the purpose of Religion in the Selknam and Yamana tribes of Tierra del Fuego and that manifested by the "tribes" of Rome, Mecca, or any other "cultic authority center"! In one of the Men's initiation rites there's an admonition that would have resonated with P.T. Barnum ... *"Never let them know!"* ... and people wonder why Pope JP2 had all his personal papers burned before he died.

Oh, once again, if you think you have a hankering to read this ... Amazon has used copies for *under a buck* ... such a deal!

Notes:

1. http://btripp-books.livejournal.com/2255.html
2. http://amzn.to/2c26i0Z

Wednesday, July 27, 2005[1]

Whew ... that took a while ...

Well, that certainly took a long time to get through ... not due to the writing or subject matter, mind you, but all the "distractions" of late. Frankly, there have been *dozens* of nights when I'd hoped to sit down with this book, but ended up passing out at the keyboard instead, so I'm glad that over the past few nights I was able to get some reading time in!

This book is the third part of the North/South/Central American myth series by John Bierhorst ... The Mythology of Mexico and Central America[2] ... which takes a very different tack than the previous two. Whereas its predecessors went tribal region by tribal region through a geographical area, this takes "themes", ranging up to "Nation-making" in how the various myths have been used to foster national identity in the various Central American states (perhaps most blatantly in the Mexican flag). It lacks the detail of the other books myth-to-myth, but provides much more cultural context ... no doubt due to the much better documented histories of the Aztecs, Maya, etc. in the region.

Again, if this "is your thing", this would make or an interesting read, as would the whole trilogy. I had one "aha" experience in this, with the history of the Virgin of Guadalupe (who is Tonantzin, the Aztec "Mother of the Gods" re-cast as a Catholic Mary), the info on which was certainly "worth the price of admission", but then again I'm always looking for factoids on how the Xtians co-opted the Old Gods!

While I am *still* plowing through Voices Of The First Day[3] (which has, admittedly gotten *much* better once I cleared the first section), I think my next "main read" is going to continue in the Native American vein and move into Dhyani Ywahoo's book on Cherokee spirituality, Voices Of Our Ancestors[4], which looks to be a pretty straight-forward peek into a particular tribal tradition. As I've noted, I have a slug of books from 10 years ago that I still need to plow through, so I'm hoping to get back to reading at least a book a week for a while now. I probably have a half-dozen titles on Native American subjects to read, so we'll see how long my interest keeps up ... I've also been eyeing some Sufi books *and* some hefty cosmology/physics tomes!

Notes:

1. http://btripp-books.livejournal.com/1825.html
2. http://amzn.to/2cNUbWn
3. http://btripp-books.livejournal.com/1385.html
4. http://btripp-books.livejournal.com/8447.html

Monday, September 5, 2005[1]

And now for something completely different ...

I finished up another book over the weekend ... this one was given to me for Father's Day and was sufficiently large (I think it's 10x10") that it kept "getting in the way", so I sort of pushed through reading it to get it out of the bathroom and onto a bookshelf! It's Weird Illinois[2] by the guys who have that new "Weird USA" show on Discovery or TLC. While it was generally an amusing read, it was heavy on "standard knowledge" ghost stories from the Chicago area, and skipped over whole categories of "weirdness" (like the "Egyptian" stuff *supposedly* discovered downstate or the *purported* Phoenician artifacts found at the mouth of the Chicago river). There were some "gee, I might want to go check that out" items in there too ... so it's not like it was pointless or anything. I guess there's a whole series of these books coming out now for quite a number of states, if you're interested.

While I'm in "review mode" I might as well touch on Valiant[3] ... which we went to see yesterday. OK ... it's animation ... it's for the kids ... it was sort of interesting. The central idea is that this little, yet brave, pigeon named Valiant wants to join the WW2 war efforts in the Homing Pigeon corps. Due to "heavy losses" he is taken on, and his mis-fit group ends up being pressed into the "most important mission". Being a Disney film, there are a lot of "names" involved as voice talents, including Ewan McGregor, Tim Curry, John Hurt, and John Cleese ... only the latter being "recognizable" to my unexpecting ear. Just over an hour long, it doesn't drag, but the only bone it throws to the adults in the audience is a parade of WW2 movie character clichés and a few bad puns ... however, there isn't much "tension" unless you're under 6 years old or have a phobia of being chased by falcons!

Notes:

1. http://btripp-books.livejournal.com/1555.html
2. http://amzn.to/2cmdwMn
3. https://goo.gl/qx0kc5

Thursday, October 27, 2005

Finally done with this one ...

Whew! I don't know how long it's been that I've been plowing through this book (OK, so the OCD made me go searching ... I started reading this in April '04), but it's been a LONG read. As has been the case with 90% of what I've been reading of late, Voices Of The First Day: Awakening In The Aboriginal Dreamtime has been sitting on my shelf for quite a while and seemed to be something that *should* have been a reasonably quick read, given my interest in the subject matter. Well, it occurred to me several times while enmired in this that *some books* should come with "warning stickers" to the effect that the author is a loony anti-Western Luddite with pronounced Green Party orientations! No matter *how* good his research into the Aboriginal life might be, if it's constantly being presented with lurid *"we must return to hunter-gatherer ways!"* freak-outs, it's likely to irritate most readers! I'll quote one particularly pungent rant:

> *We are blinded by the delusions that rise from our hollow and rotting social order. It is vain pomposity to believe that humanity can advance while the earth and its native peoples, plants, and animals are enslaved, desecrated, and destroyed. The dream of human origins and destiny as an evolution from monkeys swinging in trees to men in space suits lumbering off to other planets is an adolescent dream of uninitiated men drunk on the power of the cerebral cortex. Unfortunately, the men who maintain this dream are the ones who hold economic, military, and political power today. Whether it be by sociopolitical revolution, economic disaster, or environmental catastrophes, the overturning of this power is the only hope for the earth. The change must occur while there is still time to nurture the seed and to prepare ourselves inwardly for the dream of regeneration.*

Quite a sidetrack for a book that is *supposed* to be an in-depth look at the Aboriginal culture and spirituality. Needless to say, the author has some very specific axes to grind, most of which (if you figure out what he is ultimately proposing) involve the elimination of *billions* of people in order to enable what he frames as a "dream of regeneration"!

Not that the book was *useless*, mind you ... I found several *fascinating* bits which dove-tailed both with my Shamanic studies and my readings in advanced theories of Physics and Biology. It's just that, well, it kept coming back to tantrums over how the author felt the rest of the human race should live (in small hunter-gatherer bands, with no technology or visible culture). Now, if you're a fan of the Green Party's lunatic fringe (although I don't suppose most folks who read my journal are likely to fit that profile!), this book would no doubt make you wet your pants. For the rest of you, unless you have a very specific interest in Aboriginal Anthropology (which does, of course, get a decent share of these 391 pages), I'd say steer clear ... the book may have its redeeming qualities, but it's a bit like trying to get directions from the booze-crazed wino on the corner ... the information might not be worth putting up with the presenter!

Notes:

1. http://btripp-books.livejournal.com/1385.html
2. http://amzn.to/2cmbyva

Sunday, November 20, 2005[1]

Another one bites the dust ...

Sometimes I read books for *very* "obsessive/compulsive" reasons, and this is one of those cases. I've had this Krishnamurti book sitting around for *ages* (as those who have been keeping up with my LibraryThing catalog[2] may have noticed, I'd read several of his books back in the 90's) and had no great compulsion to read it, but I *did* start another book some weeks back which was in a very "small" format, and the two books (this[3] and this[4]) preceding it were rather large format books, so I felt a need (knowing how small books can disappear on the shelf) of pushing an intermediate-sized book to the front of the line to provide some step-down to the smaller book. Now, isn't *that* a ringing endorsement of the book?

What to say about the You Are The World[5] collection of Krishnamurti's talks? *{Oh, go ahead ... sing along ... I'm sure that Bob Geldof was inspired by this when he wrote the "We" version!}* Well, on one hand it does seem a bit *dated* as the lectures in it were presented at various American universities (Brandeis, UC Berkeley, Stanford, UC Santa Cruz) in the late 60's, with the concerns and perspectives of the time. He's also (as he mentions frequently) a very *serious* fellow, so there is a sense of him waiting with a ruler to rap the knuckles of any listeners/readers who might wish to find some levity in the proceedings! Of course, Krishnamurti is somewhat of a "tragic figure", having been "raised like veal" by the Theosophical Society in India to be some sort of "World Teacher" ... a role that he rejected in his mid-30's, when he disassociated himself from them, and insisted they shut down the "order" that had been founded to promote him. He spent the next 50-some years working as an "independent lecturer" (pretty much doing what Leonard Nemoy did with the book "I Am Not Spock"), being an "anti-Guru".

The "context" aside, Krishnamurti *is* a "deep thinker" and has given much consideration to many things, so his lectures do at least have some "meat" to them. His perspective, coming from a high Brahmin family and then being swallowed into the deepest bowels of the post-Blavatsky Theosophy movement, is, of course, unique. For me, they're more a "mental exercise" than anything ... and, in the words of a *different* philosopher, "your mileage may vary".

Notes:

1. http://btripp-books.livejournal.com/1197.html
2. http://www.librarything.com/catalog/BTRIPP
3. http://www.livejournal.com/users/btripp_books/1385.html
4. http://www.livejournal.com/users/btripp_books/1555.html
5. http://amzn.to/2ct0b6w

Wednesday, November 23, 2005[1]

A small book ...

You know when I mentioned that I was having to "step down" book sizes so a small-format book that I was reading wasn't going to "get lost on the shelf"? Well, When The Sun Moves Northward: The Way Of Initiation[2] is that small book. This is one of those charming bits of Theosophical ephemera that makes you wonder how they've stayed in print so long (in this case, from 1923). It seems that this book exists to put its author, Mabel Collins', major work *The Light On The Path* (written in 1885) in context, if a strange sort of context. Now, I've not (that I can recall) read this latter title, so I don't know if she goes into how the book was written, but in *this* book she talks about reading it written on the walls of a mystic chapel on some elevated plane. Of course, having been one of Blavatsky's associates, this doesn't seem any more or less implausible than *The Secret Doctrine* showing up scrawled out in red or blue crayon by "the masters" while H.P.B. slept!

This book primarily suffers from the habit of classic Theosophists to try to merge *genuine* mystical material with a gentrified Anglican Christianity. It swings back and forth from rather stunning observations on death or spiritual purging fires, and dainty Easter-Sunday lace-gloved pieties. Perhaps this is my *own* bias coming to the fore, but Christianity is so antagonistic to any sort of *personal* interaction with the Sacred (except in terms of their twisted fairy tale), that pulling it into a spiritual exercise is a bit like insisting the seeker take two steps back for every three they move forward! Anyway, the book describes a supposed "ritual cycle" running from December through May (Christmas through Easter), but a developmental course taken over numerous incarnations. Needless to say, "your mileage my vary" on this sort of thing.

I was interested to see that Quest Books no longer has this in its active catalog (although the edition I have was only from 1987), and that used copies via Amazon are going for as much as $21.66 (cover on this was $4.75), so it may have been one of those "released to put into circulation a few key concepts" projects that is then pulled after a short period. Again, there are some really remarkable insights in this little volume, but finding them requires a lot of sifting though stale dogmatism and over-florid prose.

Notes:

1. http://btripp-books.livejournal.com/905.html
2. http://amzn.to/2c6f2kU

Tuesday, November 29, 2005[1]

Another fast read ...

Well, *that* was fun. My current time-for-reading matrix works really well with books that have lots of little bitty sections, and I was pretty much able to knock down this one with 10 "reads" of 12 pages each! Why did I pick out Shakti Gawain's Creative Visualization[2]? Dunno. Although I will tell you that I had *two* little synchronicities involving the book over the first couple of days I was reading it (one in an L.J. post and one with something going in to my Library-Thing catalog). Frankly, I was expecting to not connect very much with this book (I've spent too long "on the Dark Side" to see much more than silliness in most "newage" stuff), however, it *IS* a very good primer for folks with no background in psi workings, with most of its exercises being both "classic" and reasonably useful (although there were some points when I'm thinking *"uh, but what do you do when somebody in the group starts having seizures and channeling Nyarlathotep?"*, not a subject oft dealt with in Fluff Bunny books!).

As folks out there with a creepy stalking mental file of all my historical details will no doubt recall, I started out in the "psychic game" fairly early in life ... having affiliated with the Foundation Church of the Millennium very soon after their schism with the (somewhat notorious) Process Church of the Final Judgement. The Process/Foundation was big into psi/healing stuff, and had several classes a week in this area. They discovered that I was a "natural" channel, and was used for "distant healing" quite a bit (where I'd "bring in" the person to be worked on). So, I was amused to find *very familiar* exercises for various healing things in this book.

I would actually recommend this book to folks looking for an introduction to "tapping into" universal forces. While I, personally, have issues with some of the low-level stuff (are there *really* people out there whose life goal is to have a new pickup truck with various accessories?), it has simple exercises for clarifying one's goals and focusing energy towards achieving them. Heck, I even picked up a new "affirmation" that I'm going to be working with!

It amuses me to think how much of this sort of stuff has "bled out" into the general consciousness, as so many of the "goal setting" sorts of exercises are all over the network marketing industry ... and, frankly, a lot of that sort of thing goes back to Napoleon Hill in the 30's ... but I'd probably point somebody new to this stuff to Creative Visualization[3] for it's "easy to get" systems before steering them to the "more difficult" Think And Grow Rich[4].

Notes:

1. http://btripp-books.livejournal.com/685.html
2-3. http://amzn.to/2cLV11N
4. http://amzn.to/2cffRFK

Tuesday, November 29, 2005[1]

why, lookie there!

Gee ... *that* doesn't happen too often, now does it? My knocking down two books in two days, and three in a week! This aberrant quirk was brought to you by a manual-feed printing project that needed my on-going, but not *constant* attention today that allowed me to read 4 pages for every thing I had to feed into the printer. Given that I'd already *started* the book, and had a couple of "reading opportunities" later in the day, I had just enough book time to finish up this one.

And, oh, those *Sufis*! Over the years I have read quite a lot of Sufi material (primarily the ISHK books, in various series), and they're always working some angle. This book, Lucy M.J. Garnett's The Dervishes Of Turkey[2] is great example. First of all, it's not *cheap:* this little 5"x7.5", 200-page book currently goes for a whopping *$35.00* on both the ISHK site and on Amazon! That certainly sets up "expectations" of the *value* of the information enclosed, doesn't it? However, countering that is a somewhat *blistering* review of it *in its own Foreword* by noted Orientalist author Omar M. Burke, including such barbs as:

> "...hundreds of books on Sufism exist, most of them completely out of tune with Sufism itself ... because there is a public for them, not because they have anything more than entertainment value"

> "... Ms. Garnett clearly has almost no knowledge of any Eastern language, certainly not of Persian, Arabic, or Turkish beyond the most elementary."

> "Other grotesque mistakes abound"

> "One of the most useful aspects of this book is to show just how near-illiterate Western writers and 'specialists' were."

> "In whole sections, there are errors on literally every page."

> "... may of the errors which appear in orientalist and other literary work during the 20th Century appear to have been copied from this book"

... and so on. Pretty odd to have a book *savaged* in its own pages, isn't it? Especially a book that they're charging a premium for. And a book that, having been originally published in 1912 would have likely faded off into obscurity long ago were it not for ISHK keeping it in print.

Ah, but this is a *Sufi* book, so things are rarely as they seem. After all, the late Idries Shah's *"The Book Of The Book"* is still in print, and for $25 you can get a nice hardcover book with a few pages of text *about* the book and then a couple of hundred blank pages. Wow, "how Zen!" ... no, just those wacky Sufis and their teaching methods. So, let's see ... the current book is very highly priced, yet is ripped apart for its many faults, yet still in print way after it should have had any impact ... what's the deal? I do, of course, have a theory.

I suspect (rather strongly) that in the pages of The Dervishes Of Turkey[3] there are a few *key concepts* that the folks at ISHK/Octagon wish to have available. Now, in reading this I found some *very interesting* points, some which would be familiar to the readers of Aleister Crowley, some that would be (oddly enough) familiar to the fans of Jack Chick's tracts, and some that just struck me as "oooh, *that's* interesting" (like the idea that there are Djins who are "spirits of the letters" which make "word magic" work). However, the one thing which I think keeps this in print is the author's discussion of the "Axis", or the one "teacher of the age" (and the various hierarchical systems below him). As many considered Idries Shah just such an "Axis" in his life, the sections in this book regarding that station might be their way of defining/promoting that stance, without having to outright declare it to be the case. Again, this is my "take" on the situation, but I'd be surprised to find that my suppositions here are too far off base!

Anyway, it's a pretty decent read, the late-1800's writing style is not such that it bogs you down, and the book is certainly full of interesting stuff. Is it worth $35 to pick up a copy? Well, I "needed it" in my collection ... however, you might be better served by borrowing a copy from your local public library.

Notes:

1. http://btripp-books.livejournal.com/264.html
2-3. http://amzn.to/2cLTRDx

Saturday, December 17, 2005[1]

Another book down ...

Sometimes a book takes a very long time to read, for no particular reason. This is one of those. I was given this book by a friend for Xmas in 1990 (it's got a note in it saying "best wishes for '91") ... and so it's been "in the mix" here for *fifteen years*. It's amazing what a different world it is between the two dates ... in December 1990, I was a top VP at a Public Relations agency, in charge of all of our conference/event projects, pulling in a six-figure salary, single (although I was dating The Wife at that point), and reading a lot ... so this book somehow feels like an artifact of a distant age!

Frankly, Dhyani Ywahoo's Voices Of Our Ancestors: Cherokee Teachings from the Wisdom Fire[2] is quite a good book, and it surprises me that she's not done a follow-up to it. I think that this is the first time that a "non-science" book has left so many questions hanging in the air for me (as I've noted in discussing previous books, I recently have been plowing through a backlog of things that were purchased 10-15 years ago, a gap which often dulls the "cutting edge" stuff quite a bit). In the book, Dhyani Ywahoo (who, according to this, is a full lineage-holder and trained teacher of her people's spiritual knowledge) seems to be setting up the foundation for a major outreach of Cherokee (or *Tsalagi*, as she uses in the book) traditional teachings via her "SunRay Meditation Society"[3], which is mentioned to have locations in many cities. I found the possibility of checking this out further enticing.

However, when I Googled SunRay, I was surprised to find that, while the organization still existed, it was pretty much in one location, which appears to primarily be a Tibetan Buddhist retreat center! Obviously, at some point since 1987 when this book came out and *now*, Ms. Ywahoo must have had some sort of "conversion experience", and seems to only now be presenting the Tsalagi teachings in some sort of mix with Nyingma and Drikung Kagyu Tibetan materials. How odd! There don't seem to be any other books by her or about her, so this book sort of leaves one hanging with the potential of the moment, which since went in other directions.

That all being said, Voices Of Our Ancestors[4] is a worthwhile read. I can't, now that I've finished it, quite put my finger on *why* it was so hard for me to get into reading this (I started the book a good half dozen times and never got past the introduction), as it's not "difficult", and not "preachy", yet I had a hard time "getting traction" with it. Go figure. The book has a nice mix of historical context, general discussion of the Tsalagi spirituality, some myth and legend, and quite a number of practical meditations and exercises. A whole system of "crystal work" is outlined, discussing the nature of various crystals, their vibrations, how they relate to bodily functions, and to cosmological forces. While the book does have a goodly amount of "chakra work" described, that's on an internal, or meditative, plane, and the author strongly warns against the "newage" use of crystals for "chakra balancing", etc. ... actually, the various specific *warnings* of "what *not* to do", were probably the most "AHA!" points in the book for me, as she clearly outlines in several instances why (within the Tsalagi system) things become hazardous. Very useful.

Anyway, I'd certainly recommend this book as a look into a Native American spiritual path. I think that it's too bad that Dhyani Ywahoo's "SunRay" group did not evolve into a far-flung teaching network for the Tsalagi tradition, but I guess (in the absence of any follow-up), this is what she feels stands on its own to present that. And, once again, if you're looking to pick it up, Amazon has a bunch of second-hand copies for under a buck, so it's something you could check out for very little investment.

Sunday, December 18, 2005[5]

Wow ... how unsettling ...

Geez ... now, *that's* a shocker. I know that from time to time "back in the day", I'd be half-way through a sci-fi novel before realizing that I'd already *read* it (a frequent possibility given a reasonably popular book might have editions out there with a dozen different covers), but it only rarely happens with non-fiction books.

I just discovered that I'd read Dhyani Ywahoo's Voices Of Our Ancestors[6] back in 1988, right after it came out! I knew there was "something about it", but I'd assumed in recent years that it had some vibe about it because it was a gift book that I was feeling guilty about not having read ... *instead* now I suspect that the "thing about it" was that it was a duplicate copy of something that was already on the shelf (with my library seal impressed in it) and that since it had a note from my friend, neither copy was really "recyclable", thereby creating a "unique status" for that book. Dang.

Needless to say, this "shock" came as I was unloading books from another shelf to log them in ... sort of a "how did *this* get *here*?" moment. Fortunately, I recently discovered a print-out from my previous attempt at cataloging my collection (which, while having less detail than the current LibraryThing catalog, at least tells me what year stuff was read) a dozen years or so back, and I was able to at least give it some context.

Interesting that I made it through that whole book without having a flash of "oh, I've read this before!" ... how bizarre.

Notes:

1. http://btripp-books.livejournal.com/8447.html
2. http://amzn.to/2c2MXOm
3. http://www.sunray.org/
4. http://amzn.to/2c2MXOm
5. http://btripp-books.livejournal.com/8552.html
6. http://amzn.to/2c2MXOm

Tuesday, December 20, 2005[1]

A quick read ...

What a strange little book ... being both strange *and* little for the same reason ... I don't know what the impetus was for putting this out (now in a revised edition, even) rather than "fleshing it out" into a more substantial volume, but there it is. It would be "little" at its nominal 140 pages, but what reduces that, *and* makes it "strange" is that it's half in English and half in Spanish, with 3 pages of "only English" up front (title page, CR page, TOC) and 3 pages of "only English" (references) in the back, leaving 134 pages to be split between two languages, essentially a 67-page book. Why?

Eduardo El Curandero: The Words of a Peruvian Healer[2] is obviously a follow-up to Douglas Sharon's definitive (and very rare) Wizard of the Four Winds: A Shaman's Story[3], but it appears to be based on "out-takes" from some of Richard Cowan's filming of Don Eduardo ... and just seems *odd* for that reason. The "revised edition" (the original came out in 1982, this in 1999), was no doubt due to commemorate the passing of Don Eduardo in 1996 ... perhaps they felt this was a more approachable book than *Wizard*, and could reach more people, but from somebody *familiar* with the subject matter, well ... I wanted a few hundred more pages!

Now, as background, I studied with Don Eduardo Calderon in Peru in the 80's ... and my "main Shamanic teacher", Dr. Alberto Villoldo, was for many years Don Eduardo's prime student. As such, any book that "brings him back to life" for me is a treat, as Eduardo was a special person, and I regret that I was only able to spend the few weeks that I did with him. It is interesting that Don Eduardo seemed to have *two* key "fan clubs" from the First World ... there is the side of Alberto Villoldo, who came to totally immerse himself in the *Shamanism* of Don Eduardo, and then you have the Sharons, who seemingly never dropped the "We're Cultural Anthropologists And We're Doing Important Research Here" mask. Frankly, I don't think either side had much use for the other ... Sharon never mentions Villoldo in any of the books, yet Alberto spent *decades* at Eduardo's elbow, and there's even a sniffing "dig" at "new age practitioners" in the introduction here, something no doubt aimed at Alberto.

Ah, I could go on about that stuff ... but I should get back to the book.

If one has an interest in taking a peek into a living Shamanic tradition, Eduardo El Curandero[4] could be a good introduction. It's (as noted) brief, has a *lot* of pictures (from the film out-takes), and gives a good sense of Don Eduardo as a person, a part of his culture, and as a Shaman.

One of the most interesting things in this book (for me, at least), was a look at Don Eduardo's "mesa" (his ritual equipment) with photos of it in the early '70s and 1989, with a item-by-item inventory of what's there and what it was used for by Eduardo. A version of this was in Sharon's *Wizard* (from 1978), but it's approached a bit differently here. Of course, for one of Don Eduardo's students, who had had opportunity to "work with" various staffs and elements of his mesa, it's exciting to "touch" that vibration again ... especially seeing (in the 1989 photo) Eduardo's late-period *seguro*, a bottle of "stuff" in which the Quechuan Shamans "carry their lineage", and with which new students are initiated into that lineage. So cool!

Unlike some of the books reviewed here, this one is relatively new, so hasn't slid into that "fabulous deal" range via the Amazon used vendors ... but you could still score a copy for about ten bucks (with shipping) if you were so inclined.

Notes:

1. http://btripp-books.livejournal.com/8930.html
2. http://amzn.to/2cFW9UD
3. http://amzn.to/2cduclD
4. http://amzn.to/2cFW9UD

Friday, December 23, 2005[1]

Another fast read ...

Ah, back in the day ... an odd factoid occurred to me when reading this book ... I must have been *some sort of nerd* back in high school and into college, as I actually *subscribed* to Biblical Archaeology Review (the publishers of this volume), and not only did I have a *subscription*, but I had bought all the back issues, so I had a complete set! You see, my *dislike* of Christianity is *not* ill-informed, but the product of looking closely at something (like the making of sausages and laws) that is better served by being unobserved.

This book, The Dead Sea Scrolls: After Forty Years[2] is a record of a symposium held at the Smithsonian back in 1990 by Hershel Shanks (of B.A.R.) along with a number of the Dead Sea Scrolls researchers. This has, of course, "aged" on my shelf (it would be "After Fifty Five Years" at this point!), but, unlike some of the cutting edge science stuff, I don't think this has gotten any staler by the delay in reading it. The book is pretty brief (under 100 pages) and straight forward, having five sections, one by each of the seminar presenters, plus a final panel discussion .

Being the "anti-Christian" kind of guy I am, I really appreciate anything that makes the Biblical Literalists look like idiots, and this sort of *scholarly* study of the Bible and its origins is a breath of fresh air. One of the researchers even addresses the "lay folk (who) still want to think of the Bible as somehow *inerrant*" as being particularly ignorant of the "fluidity" of both the canon and the contents thereof over the early centuries of the Christian Era, and earlier. One of the things I found *fascinating* in this was the rather late period when the *Jewish* scriptures became "set", and even then having content differences depending on region.

There are all sorts of interesting tidbits in this, like how we know *nothing* of the actual sectarian beliefs of the Pharisees and Sadducees, despite how prominently the *names* of these groups feature in the New Testament, yet for a group that has nearly *no* Biblical role, the Essenes, there is this whole library of texts! Gotta love those little ironies.

I must say, having read this has set me to thinking about checking out some other books ... I'd been familiar with John Allegro's "post-scroll" work (classics like The Sacred Mushroom and the Cross[3], which I'd tried to get the rights to for an Eschaton re-print), and there were a couple of "knocks" against him in here which made me want to go looking for his "unauthorized release" of the fabled Copper Scroll.

Anyway ... needless to say, a book of lectures on 2,000-year-old text fragments is not everybody's cup of tea, but it's been one of my long-time "areas of interest", so I found this quite the interesting read. As one might expect, this doesn't have a ton of folks lining up to buy it, so if it sounds like something you'd want to pick up, you're in luck as Amazon has "like new" copies of The Dead Sea Scrolls: After Forty Years[4] in their "Used and New" listings for as little as 1¢!

Notes:

1. http://btripp-books.livejournal.com/9112.html
2. http://amzn.to/2c2IpaH
3. http://amzn.to/2cFUxui
4. http://amzn.to/2c2IpaH

Monday, December 26, 2005[1]

Another book ... one EVERYBODY should check out!

OK, so it's Xmas and all ... and I don't *really* want to get into a whole bunch of L.J. *drama*, so if you're one of the "Left-Leaning" folks who read my journal, it would probably behoove you to just skip the rest of this review. I'm not planning on "ranting and raving", but I'm probably going to be saying some stuff that will get your knickers all knotted, and who needs that right after all the Holiday feasting, right?

I had Unfit For Command[2] *highly* recommended to me by polaris93[3], after she'd read it (and reviewed it[4] in her journal). I'd sort of chided her on her sense of *amazement* at some of the details (as most of the "dirty laundry" had been aired extensively on the web during the last election), but, having now read this book, it *is* AMAZING the depths of scheming depravity that John Kerry plumbed in his sordid career.

Now, as long-time readers of this space know, I do *not* understand the Left ... much as I do not understand most Christians ... because 90% of what they believe in is based on blatant, outright, and poorly-concealed LIES ... lies that any sensible person looking at the situation would say a hearty "WTF??" over. And yet they are blind to the deceits of their "leaders", and willing to paint their "enemies" with the same tar with which they are so thickly covered.

I wish every American would read Unfit For Command[5] about John Kerry, Dereliction of Duty[6] about Bill Clinton, and Ann Coulter's remarkable book Treason[7] for a look at how the Democratic Party came to not just be "the opposition" to the GOP, but has become a Fifth Column dedicated to aiding and abetting "all enemies foreign and domestic" to the detriment of the United States of America. Just these three books should give *anybody* pause about the nature of the current political landscape ... after all, John Kennedy, by today's standards, would be *to the right* of George Bush on most issues, when did the Democratic Party turn into a neo-Stalinist revolutionary front?

One tidbit in Unfit For Command[8] that I found absolutely *fascinating*, and had, remarkably, not heard previously, was from an interview with a former KGB bigwig who outlined the level of control that Moscow had over the "anti-war" movement in the 60's and 70's ... even to laughingly saying that he should have been given credit by Kerry for writing his Fulbright Committee testimony, as virtually every "detail" in what Kerry was presenting to the Congress had been invented by KGB propagandists in his office! I don't know if John Kerry is/was a Communist per se, but he certainly has put his own personal agenda above the interests of his country at every turn ... and not just as "opinion", as there have been actions which, judged *honestly* and not through the far-left filter of the MSM, are *treasonous* at face value, no "spin" needed!

It's a tragedy that there aren't more Joe Liebermans out there (to cite the *only* "name" I can think of that doesn't require spitting on the ground) ... because all the Democrats seem to come up with are either criminals like the Clintons, Ted Kennedy, and John Kerry, or *lunatic* Leftists like Howard Dean, Barbara Boxer, and the rest of that sorry lot.

As you know, I'm not a *huge* fan for George W. Bush, but thank The Gods that he's President now, and not either of the scumbags he defeated. I challenge anybody to read Unfit For Command[9] with an open mind and not be glad that John Kerry is not "at the helm" of our nation! Lucky for you, this can be had for as little as 1¢ via Amazon's "new & used" service (that's what I paid!), and I *highly recommend* you checking it out.

Notes:

1. http://btripp-books.livejournal.com/9341.html
2. http://amzn.to/2c2GtiH
3. http://polaris93.livejournal.com/
4. http://www.livejournal.com/users/polaris93/232950.html
5. http://amzn.to/2c2GtiH
6. http://amzn.to/2ch9jcl
7. http://amzn.to/2c1Kdhp
8-9. http://amzn.to/2c2GtiH

Thursday, December 29, 2005[1]

Another book ...

The Wife's eldest nephew (now in his 30's) has been a big fan of Henry Rollins for *ages*, and he got me a copy of Get In The Van: On The Road With Black Flag[2] for Xmas. Now, I'm a few years older than Henry, and, while being *aware* of Black Flag, I was never that much of a "fan" (although I did have a couple of their albums), and never went to see them live.

The concept of this books is interesting, in that Rollins starts up a journal where he initially jots down a few sentences about what's going on every day or so, and this grows into longer (if less frequent) postings as the years go on (no doubt aided by having *Spin* tab him early on for a column). On one hand, it's a rather strange little window onto the history of Black Flag, but it really is more "watch Henry learn to write", especially looking back from a point where Rollins is perhaps better known as a "spoken word" performer.

The book is broken up into yearly "chapters" (with monthly sections that have the various daily postings), going from 1981 when Rollins was simply a fan of Black Flag being somewhat serendipitously added as the new singer (I'm not sure, but he was either the third or fourth lead singer for the band, replacing Dez Cadena who was wanting to switch off to just playing guitar), and on through the end of the band in 1986. It's funny reading it this way, again, from a place 20-some years down the line, as pretty much what he was going for back then was a "blog", but was keeping it on scraps of paper rather than via something like LiveJournal.

Get In The Van[3] is not a *comfortable* book to read, as it is primarily a vehicle for Henry to deal with his demons, and there is a lot of rage and loathing involved. Needless to say, the boy had "issues", which evolve as the book moves on, but very few get "resolved". This is also a look at what crappy conditions bands like Black Flag had to tour in back then ... he's always hungry, always sleep deprived, always dealing with some physical issue. However, his antipathy for the "straight world" is such that he keeps going back to preferring touring over anything else. His hatred of Cops is a common thread for these aspects, and is another thing which makes this an "uncomfortable" read.

Frankly, I wished there was more "dishing" and less ranting ... the "name dropping" bits come and go, almost off-handed, and it's fascinating (especially for somebody who was pretty much into the Punk scene back in those days) to hear who was hanging with who, who was working on side projects with who, etc. I would think that this would also be a big disappointment for Black Flag fans, as there is more Henry saying "well, fuck them" than really detailing the inner workings of the band.

As a guy who's been "clean and sober" for a couple of decades, it was interesting to watch Rollins process his angst and rage without the "benefit" of booze and drugs (things that he is violently against), so contrary to the "rock

& roll lifestyle" cliché, albeit his use of physical pain as a way to process psychological pain is in itself a cliché (no doubt familiar to any LiveJournal reader), which could be argued is as "weak" as using substance abuse to distance oneself from what one is feeling.

Oh, also ... if this sounds like something you'd want to check out, make sure to get the *Second Edition* (published in 2004) of the book rather than the original 1994 version (not that one would be more likely to run across the older one, but still) as there is supposed to be a LOT more stuff (photos, copies of flyer art, etc.) in this one, as well as the various corrections and text additions that one would expect from a second edition (although, I must admit, I found a good half dozen outright *typos* in this). Again, this is a book that I wouldn't necessarily recommend to *everybody*, but if you have an interest in the band, the time, or Rollins (or the psychology of the struggling rock performer), it would be well worth the read.

Notes:

1. http://btripp-books.livejournal.com/9606.html
2-3. http://amzn.to/2c1GQqN

Thursday, December 29, 2005[1]

The quickest sort of read ...

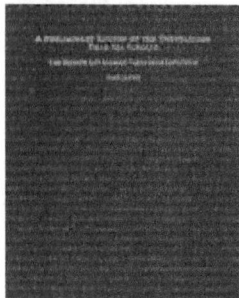

O.K., so this one is almost "cheating" ... I'd gotten this about the same time as the Dead Sea Scrolls book that I finished (and reviewed) a week ago, but I didn't realize at the time I ordered it that it ... well ... that it wasn't really *in English*! Yes, the Foreword and Introduction and various editorial bits are in English, but the other 120 or so pages of the book consist of printouts of 1st Century Hebrew and Aramaic texts ... neither of which I can even begin to decipher! Needless to say, I'd sort of *assumed* that there would have been some translation involved, but that's not the case, no doubt due to the "scholarly audience" for which A Preliminary Edition Of The Unpublished Dead Sea Scrolls: The Hebrew And Aramaic Texts From Cave Four - Fascicle One[2] was intended.

As anyone familiar with the Dead Sea Scrolls is aware, there are some really twisted "academic politics" involved with their publication. Various texts were "assigned" to a small group of experts back in the 50's, and the vast majority of these texts have not as yet been officially published. This current volume was sort of produced "on the sly", having been based on a concordance of texts which listed all the *words* in the Cave 4 material (which was all very fragmentary, possibly having been intentionally destroyed by Roman troops at the time of the suppression of the Qumran community associated with them). The concordance, while not reproducing any of the texts themselves, did list all the words in the texts and the words that appeared on either side of them. Obviously, in the 1950's this was a pretty locked-down way of providing *some* information, but the "author" of this volume, Ben Zion Wacholder, wondered what would happen (in the late 80's) if he fed the data into a computer. Remarkably, a very coherent set of texts resulted from this experiment, and he decided that he would publish this outside the purview of the "official" Scroll teams. Again, there has been a very high level of scholarly frustration with the speed at which the Dead Sea Scroll material has been being released, so, as put in the opening words of Hershel Shanks' Foreword *"This is a historic book."*, allowing researchers access to materials that might have languished under jealous control for decades or more.

I, of course, don't have the linguistic tools necessary to really make use of this book, but was eager to get a copy, as rare as the source material is. Needless to say, I wouldn't suggest that anybody run out to get their own copy of A Preliminary Edition Of The Unpublished Dead Sea Scrolls[3] unless you are a 1st Century Biblical scholar (and I'd suspect that were you one, you would have already picked up a copy of this in the 15 years since it appeared!) ... but it is a fascinating thing to have.

Notes:
1. http://btripp-books.livejournal.com/9839.html
2-3. http://amzn.to/2cFLWrf

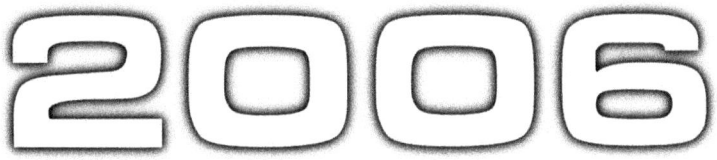

Monday, January 9, 2006[1]

Another book ...

(sigh) ... I had really *hoped* that this book was going to be better than it ended up being. Not, mind you, that it was *bad* or a dull read, or difficult, or anything like that, it's just that *for me* it was pretty much re-packaging a lot of stuff that I'd read before in other contexts. Now, admittedly, I have read *a lot* of books over the years in the general ballpark of <u>At the Heart of the Web: The Inevitable Genesis of Intelligent Life</u>[2], so I shouldn't expect great revelations (especially in a book that came out 16 years ago), but I was hoping that the author, George A. Seielstad, would take it *beyond* the "usual suspects" of cosmological and biological niches. Frankly, he *does* tease the reader with the concept that Man is evolving in his particular technological manner in order to be able to take "Gaian life" beyond the bounds of the Mother planet ... but he never *quite* gets there.

If you want a book that firmly puts Man in context of the greater cosmos, <u>At the Heart of the Web</u>[3] is a good one for providing all the various charts and graphs, showing various levels of being, natures of stars, size and lifespan of creatures, etc.. etc., etc. ... while providing all the details of the Anthropic stance ... how things are "just so" from the microcosmic forces to the expansion factors of the Universe in general. He *does* have nuggets of info that I'd previously not been aware (there were some "Johnny Carson" moments where I was thinking *"I did **not** know that!"*) like if the Earth somehow managed to collapse down to a black hole it would have an event horizon that would be about 1/3 of an inch across, and that it appears that the Universe "prefers" to have an ever-reducing number of super-massive black holes, and that the mathematics of ultra-super-massive black holes end up with them eventually exploding, and that the math for a black hole that had the entire mass of the known Universe exploding would be virtually identical with the math involved in the Big Bang (i.e., the concept of the "recycling Universe").

In some aspects this is a very "green" book, firmly rooted in the "Gaian hypothesis" of the Earth being one "superorganism" of inter-related parts, of which Humanity is sort of the "fruiting body", ready to move out into space. However, it is sort of difficult to see where the author "is coming from" in those areas, as most of the time when he's meandering over into that zone, it's in the form of charts and graphs and not polemics (well, right up to the last chapter, which I had hoped was going to point to space, but instead got tut-tutty over Human, and especially Western/developed nations' stewardship of planetary resources).

If nothing else, <u>At the Heart of the Web</u>[4] gives background for *why* there is an "anthropic principle", showing how intelligent life (like that of Man) is likely a *necessary* development of a Universe of the sort we find ourselves in. As noted above, this is certainly an *interesting* look at the various macro-

and micro-cosmic aspects to this (and the book is quite extensively illustrated, with everything from side-by-side deep space pics showing a supernova's explosion to a busted chair illustrating increasing entropy!), but I just wish the author had taken it a bit further down various *speculative* paths.

As is often the case for these books off my long-ignored "to be read" shelves, this can be had for quite little over at Amazon ... with "like new" used copies going for under a buck. Quite the deal if you'd be interested in checking this out.

Notes:

1. http://btripp-books.livejournal.com/10227.html
2-4. http://amzn.to/2bSTvMu

Monday, January 23, 2006[1]

WOOT! ... finally finished this one!

O.K ... as I've noted before, I've had this book "in process" for a very long time. I first started reading it *many* years ago, and it ended up "getting buried" in a stack of other stuff in my office ... only coming to light in my recent efforts to log my library into LibraryThing[2]. I was (going from the bookmark placement) not quite half done with this when I found it, so opted to go back to the beginning to read it again ... and I certainly found out why it had ended up in a "put aside" area!

Barbara Thiering's Jesus & the Riddle of the Dead Sea Scrolls[3] is a *fascinating* study, but it is also a very uneven read. The book runs almost 450 pages, but the "main part" (before the various appendixes) is only 160 pages This first third is well done, interesting, and quite eye-opening in the things that Thiering claims that a "technical" reading of the Qumran scroll materials, in conjunction with Biblical sources and other apocrypha, says about the events and realities of Jesus' life.

However, the first appendix, on "Chronology" (almost another third of the book) is like hitting a brick wall. This section covers the various sorts of calendars used by competing pre-Christian cults in the area, how they cycled in relation to each other, how they were adjusted so things stayed where they were supposed to be, a breakdown on "code words" relating to calendrical concepts which appear in the Bible, scrolls, etc., and a sometimes day-by-day walk-through of the events running from 9 BC to 64 AD. This section was *painful* to plow through!

Slightly less onerous is the "Locations" appendix which fleshes out the theory that most of the events of the Gospels happened in and around Qumran, and not actually in the places a "Biblical Literalist" would assume. Although I was approaching this with a lot of *"yeah, yeah, whatever"*, it does present a coherent structure where a lot of the "how could that happen?" stuff in the Bible sounds implausible. Also interesting is the "Hierarchy" appendix which discusses who was in what group and how these various cults/roles functioned.

The "cut to the chase" version of Jesus & the Riddle of the Dead Sea Scrolls[4] is that Jesus was one of many players in a "Jewish Millennialist" movement that had been started by Herod, with plans to expand out a Jewish theocratic Empire to eventually challenge Rome. There were various sects, some that were open to Gentiles, some that wanted to forcibly confront the Romans, and all of these were tied into various cults (such as the Essenes) whose Millennialism dated back at least to the Maccabees. Two main camps existed, with a fluid mix of groups between them, those being the "Eastern" (being more strict about Jewish law and asceticism), and the "Western" which eventually welcomed non-Jews and women even into the priestly (Levite) functions. Generally speaking the "Western" groups eventually morphed into Christianity, and the "Eastern" groups left behind the Dead Sea Scrolls.

The method that Thiering uses to arrive at this rather non-traditional read of the New Testament milieu is called the "pesher" technique, a word that in the Old Testament is used to denote such things as dream interpretation, but in this case (as it is set out in certain of the Scrolls), it means a systematic way of extracting a deliberately-encoded subtext from a document. As the New Testament books and the Dead Sea Scrolls came out from the same set of mystical groups, the reading methods outlined for the latter work for the former, with rather surprising results. According to the strict ascetic traditions of the "Eastern" groups, Jesus was illegitimate, having been conceived at the wrong time in the calendar (according to a very strict rule that "The Davids" such as Joseph were under), so was unable to hold any of the higher offices (which they claimed to legitimately fall to James), the "Western" groups held that since Jesus was conceived within the ritual process of betrothal and weddings, he was legitimate ... neither group even suggested "divinity" for Jesus beyond that of being a hereditary "David" (the "spirit" that came to Mary *was* Joseph in a ritual appellation!).

Anyway, it's an interesting read, and, frankly, it's the MOST PLAUSIBLE READING OF CHRISTIANITY that I've ever encountered. As many readers of this space know, I have no use for Christianity in general, and this is the only thing I've ever read that makes sense of the source materials behind all the fairy tails and priestcraft (well, except perhaps for Baigent, Leigh, and Lincoln's *The Messianic Legacy*[5]). Like the B/L/L books, Jesus doesn't actually *die* on the cross, but survives, and with political changes ends up a major player in the growth of "Christianity" in Rome, which he escapes from in the days of Nero (Paul, according to the *pesher* even writes of Jesus's escape in his final letters before he and Peter are executed), and moves with Mary M. and the kids (several) to a Herodian estate in the south of France (ah ... perhaps the "Sion" secret is the burial place of Jesus?).

Obviously, this is another of those books that I really wish all Christians would read. I hate seeing so many otherwise functional human beings throw away their lives believing in fairy tales intended for the intellectually challenged. Unlike a lot of the books I've reviewed here, this one, while not available new, is pretty pricey on the used listings ... with a "like new" copy setting you back at least $8 before shipping ... but it's definitely worth it if you want to rip off the veils of 2,000 years of lies and take a non-delusional look at what produced Christianity!

Notes:

1. http://btripp-books.livejournal.com/10488.html
2. http://www.librarything.com/catalog/BTRIPP
3-4. http://amzn.to/2cuwl8B
5. http://amzn.to/2cacvbz

Friday, January 27, 2006[1]

Another book ...

Well, this was a remarkably quick read. When I got into it I figured it to be a couple of weeks of a chapter (handily 12-18 pages each) a day or so, but I had some chunks of time (like taking The Girls off to Chuck E. Cheese last night) to fill, so managed to buzz right through this.

James Trefil's Reading the Mind of God: In Search of the Principle of Universality[2] is set up as a survey of how the idea of "universality" became established. This is the concept that the physical Laws that we are able to measure here on Earth are the same all across the Universe, and have been constant through all of time. While the idea ... that, for example, if you drop a rock on Mars (or drop a rock on some planet around a distant star) that rock will fall according to our understanding of the force of Gravity ... is hardly a shocker to our current world-view, this was not always the case. What Trefil does with this book is walk the reader through a series of discoveries/developments by scientists in various areas (Issac Newton, Edmond Halley, William Herschell, Joseph Fraunhofer, Gustav Kirchhoff & Robert Bunsen, Niels Bohr, Pieter Zeerman, Sir Joseph Norman Lockyer, John William Strutt Lord Rayleigh & Sir William Ramsay, James Hutton, Sir Charles Lyell, William Thompson Lord Kelvin, Arthur Eddington, Hans Bethe, Edwin Hubble, Alan Guth, and others) via concise thumbnails of their individual bios and work. The research goes in four basic areas, from gravity out into space, into the inner workings of Earth, to the functioning of the Sun and other stars, then to the structure of the atom and its constituent parts, and finally back towards the Big Bang, at each point showing how the idea of "universal physical laws" was built up.

This is a lot of material to pump into a 218-page book, but Reading the Mind of God[3] is hardly a "dense read", focusing on the *people* who discovered the various bits and pieces, it has more the feel of a good biography, if of an idea rather than one person. Trefil also approaches his subject with a lot of humor, poking fun at various stereotypes, and even some of the scientists he profiles (noting that "ability and humanity" are not necessarily correlated). He throws in some very good "word pictures" which I don't think I'd encountered previously (like, if an atom's nucleus was a bowling ball on your desk, the atoms would be a handful of sand buzzing around many miles away ... a great way to envision how MOST of what we know as the physical world is nothing but empty space!), as well as some "random factoids" that were new to me (i.e., the quantum fluctuation from the void which triggered the big bang probably only involved 22lbs of matter!).

Obviously, with cramming so many ideas into so few pages, a lot of details get "glossed over", and the one thing I found irritating about the book was that Trefil wouldn't just say "we have no room to delve into that here", but would throw in an aside or a footnote saying that the information on that was in such-and-such of his *other* books. I suppose that is a small matter, but I wanted to smack him every time that came up.

If you're looking to brush up on a LOT of science history in a quick read, I'd definitely recommend this book ... it is, if nothing else, a good way to become conversant on the who/what/where/when/why basics on 20 or so key figures in the development of our current understanding of science! Its theme of "universality" is also an interesting approach, as it is something which most folks probably don't have a specific conception of, yet the principle underlies much of the modern scientific world-view. And, again, as this is an "older" volume (from 1989), you can get it for cheap over on Amazon ... with "very good" copies going for as little as 45¢.

Notes:

1. http://btripp-books.livejournal.com/10733.html
2-3. http://amzn.to/2bSPPKX

Sunday, February 5, 2006[1]

Another book ...

Just as the last book reviewed here was a sort of a collection of stories of scientists whose work built up our present understanding of "universality", this is a look at some of the major archaeological discoveries of the past couple of hundred years that have shaped our understanding of human history.

Lawrence H. Robbins wrote Stones, Bones, and Ancient Cities[2] as an over-view text for his intro college courses. In it he looks at the research into the evolution of *homo sapiens* from previous ancestors, early man's rock/cave art from around the world, the development of burials (from early Neandertals to Tutankhamen), the search for lost cities (Troy, Pompeii, Machu Picchu, etc.), underwater archaeology (from the depths of Chichen Itza's "well of sacrifice" to raising Henry VIII's *Mary Rose*), how astronomical concepts fit into cultures (from Stonehenge to Chaco Canyon), and how written records have opened up windows into the past. In this he outlines the contributions of dozens of adventurers and archaeologists, both professional and amateur. Many of the stories focus on "mavericks" whose theories were far outside of the scientific mainstream of their day ... or, as he writes of Champollion (translator of the Rosetta Stone) *"(he) fit the mold of other scholarly pioneers ... who, through exceptional dedication to an elusive goal, were able to fulfill their youthful dreams"* (as several of the people profiled had been inspired early by reading myths or histories).

Unlike James Trefil's Reading the Mind of God[3], however, Robbins' Stones, Bones, and Ancient Cities[4] doesn't "build" to a central concept, but skips around from type of research to type of research, which, while informative on a point-by-point basis, does feel slightly aimless. Ultimately, though, there was little in this that I had not encountered before in other reading, so perhaps its intent as a "primer" for the uninformed led to my lack of enthusiasm for it.

Frankly, I "stumbled across" Stones, Bones, and Ancient Cities[5] on one of my to-be-read shelves while doing some tidying up for the logging in of my LibraryThing catalog[6], and I only "slotted it in" my reading queue because it had the "structural similarity" to the previous book (I actually am "in" a couple of other books at the moment as well, but thought that this would be an interesting follow-up to the previous reviewed volume). Unfortunately, the "drag factor" in this has made me question the follow-up books I had been planning on getting into, so might have to veer off into some "other directions" for a while to give the "science history" parts of my brain a breather!

Anyway, unlike many of the sitting-on-the-shelf-for-10-years books I've reviewed here, this one is still in print (probably due to being used in college courses) in a paperback edition ... although you could get a copy of this hardcover one via Amazon's "new & used" listings for a couple of bucks were you interested in checking it out.

Notes:
1. http://btripp-books.livejournal.com/10870.html
2. http://amzn.to/2bZ8vYg
3. http://btripp-books.livejournal.com/10733.html
4-5. http://amzn.to/2bZ8vYg
6. http://www.librarything.com/catalog/BTRIPP

Thursday, February 9, 2006[1]

Book ...

I was feeling a bit "over-science" with the past two books and was looking on the to-be-read shelves for something that would be "fast and light", and grabbed this one. I (as is generally the case) had this sitting around for ten plus years, and didn't really have big expectations for it (on top of the fact that all the forward-looking charts were already out of date).

However, Nigel Pennick's The Pagan Book of Days[2] surprised me. Sub-titled "A Guide to the Festivals, Traditions, and Sacred Days of the Year", it was chock full of interesting bits of info. Pennick is an Englishman who is tied into the local traditions of East Anglia, and many of the things highlighted are specifically British, but fascinating in that he is able to date when long-running traditions disappeared (a number with the advent of WW1, others in WW2, and others as late as the 1950's). There are also various calendars outlined (the "Celtic Tree Calendar" and the Runic half-months) and information on how daily cycles (specific influences on the hours) are used within yearly cycles.

Pennick also draws heavily on the Roman tradition, and it's amazing to see what "deities" were used to personify various things (such as June 8, the festival of *consciousness*, personified by the goddess "Mens"). The book (the bulk of which is just monthly listings of days and what's associated with them) is also liberally sprinkled with "Egyptian Days", which (like our own "Friday the 13th") are days of ill omen ... although for most he doesn't specify how or why they gained that attribution. There are tons of illustrations, largely classical drawings, but also featuring some very interesting sigils for phases of the calendar, some of which I'd not previously encountered.

There were plenty of "I did *not* know that!" moments in the book, although some I took with a grain or two of salt (for instance: *"The Gnostic followers of St. Nicholas, the Nicolaites, taught that the only way to salvation lay through frequent sexual intercourse."* ... talk about finding something special in one's stockings!) ... more often, though, these ran to obscure connections of deities (such at the patron goddess of the sacred hot springs at Bath, Sulis, being a manifestation of Neptune's wife Salacia) which may or may not be on particularly solid ground.

All in all, I found The Pagan Book of Days[3] quite the pleasant surprise ... nowhere near as "fluffy" as I had anticipated, although having a lot of information (all the calendrical systems, for instance) that was of minimal personal use to me. If this sounds like something that you need in your library, Amazon can hook you up with a "new" copy (via their new/used service) for a few bucks.

Notes:

1. http://btripp-books.livejournal.com/11017.html

2-3. http://amzn.to/2cug2Ot

Monday, February 13, 2006[1]

A Superb Book ...

Wow. I've read a *lot* of Sufi books over the years (over at LibraryThing I've got the 2nd most Idries Shah books in my catalog[2], at 28 titles, and those are just the ones *he* penned), but the vast majority of them are *indirect*, either simply presenting teaching stories, or hiding gems of info in the midst of "noise". This is the first one that really struck me as being "direct", laying out the how, what and why of Sufi teachings.

Of course, this makes me wonder *why* this book seems so different from all the other books, and what might be happening with this particular title that is, perhaps, indirect in its seeming directness! Such is the downfall of the student who is working just with texts and without any guide, I suppose (perhaps it is time for me to write a request to The Society for Sufi Studies).

Anyway, Sufi Thought and Action[3] is "An Anthology of Important Papers" assembled by the late great Idries Shah, including an introductory essay by himself. Shah was, by nearly unanimous regard, the "Light of the Age", the foremost Sufi teacher over the past half century. His efforts in *publishing* legitimate Sufi material (through Octagon Books, the ISHK, the ICR, and Designist Communications, among others) is referenced frequently here as being of major importance.

The book is assembled in nine sections: "Sufi Spiritual Rituals and Beliefs" by Shah, "Sufi Principles and Learning Methods" comprising 7 papers, "Current Sufi Activity" with nine subjects by one author, "Ritual, Initiation and Secrets in Sufi Circles" with 3 author's pieces, each covering 5-7 topics, "Theories, Practices and Training Systems of a Sufi School" by one author, "Key Concepts in Sufi Understanding" comprising of three papers, "Visits to Sufi Centers" with pieces by five authors, "The Sufis of Today" by one author, and "In a Sufi Monastery, and Other Papers" with seven assorted reports. It almost "feels" like Shah had gone back into the archives (I believe that I may have read some of these previously, either in other collections on in the old Designist monograph series) and pulled out the most direct not-beating-around-the-bush papers for this collection. Even topics such as the *mundane* use of ESP communications by "real Sufis" is addressed off-hand (in the context of attempting to get in touch with "supposed" Sufi teachers), as though this should be no surprise to the reader. Again, it is a remarkably "open" approach for a book from Octagon!

While this book, like most of what I've been reading over the past couple of years, has spent a decade or more on my shelf (it was published in 1990), it has the advantage of being from ISHK/Octagon, and so is still very much in print. However, this *does* mean that if you want to get a copy you're going to have to dig deeper than is often the case on the things I'm reviewing. You can get a good used copy for around $3.50, but a new one will set you back $22.00 (for a 280-page paperback).

I don't know if this would be something that I'd recommend for an *introductory* book on Sufi teachings, but if you've read some Sufi materials and were more confused than enlightened by that reading, I would *definitely* recommend checking out Sufi Thought and Action[4].

Notes:

1. http://btripp-books.livejournal.com/11442.html
2. http://www.librarything.com/catalog/BTRIPP
3-4. http://amzn.to/2cugfkA

Wednesday, February 15, 2006[1]

A short read ...

Not that it *matters*, but this is the 1,500th book logged in to my LibraryThing catalog[2] ... I'd gotten up into the "fourteen-nineties" when I finished up those other bookshelves a week or so back, but hadn't felt like "artificially" pushing over that line, so have been letting the newly-read books total up to get there!

This book, Urban Legends and the Japanese Tale[3] by David Schaefer, is the 29th title in the Institute for Cultural Research's monograph series. Frankly, I'm not sure *why* this one was not in with the others (I'd read most of the first 28 in the early 90's), but I found it in the to-be-read shelves the other day, and figured I'd pop it in while I was "on the topic". The ICR was another of Idries Shah's "projects", which began in the mid-60's in London, holding various lectures and seminars, papers from which began appearing in 1970 (I found that they're up to #46 with two new titles last year). The ICR Monographs (as well as the Designist Communications "Sufi research" series) were some of my inspirations on getting into publishing ... most of their titles are in saddle-stitched "chapbook" format (which I found appealing as a way to get a lot of information into circulation "fast and cheap") ... unfortunately, I discovered that The Publishing World really hates "chapbooks", and it takes somebody like Shah to make these sort of things *work*! Anyway, I am quite fond of these small volumes, as they always are informational, and often quite eye-opening, as it were.

Urban Legends and the Japanese Tale[4] doesn't fail on this count, relating the Web-ubiquitous "urban legend" to literary predecessors, especially in the Japanese *setsuwa* stories (although specific urban legend "story patterns" can likewise be found in the writings of Chaucer, Hawthorne, and Thoreau, to mention a few the author cites). The form of the "urban legend" can be related to "ghost stories" and "joke stories" within a spectrum of "moral stories", as all of these have some general descriptive elements in common. As this particular study came out in 1990, it obviously misses the whole *internet* aspect of the spread of these stories ... and it would be interesting to see how the author would frame the current ability of *one idiot* spreading some made-up piece of crap to *millions* in a matter of days.

One of the daunting things about the ICR Monographs is that they've *never* been cheap ... this 32-page saddle-stitched chapbook goes for $6.00 (OK, so my own poetry editions go for $5.00 in the same format, but they usually have 50-some pages!) ... and they're pretty much all still in print (except for #13 and #14 which have disappeared from all the listings, and must have been pulled early as I don't have them from 15+ years ago), so there aren't a lot of deep discount deals out there ... however, if you find "Urban Legends" an interesting subject, you might want to pick up a copy of this.

Notes:
1. http://btripp-books.livejournal.com/11770.html
2. http://www.librarything.com/catalog/BTRIPP
3-4. http://amzn.to/2cu602G

Thursday, February 16, 2006[1]

A long time coming ...

I attended the Parliament of the World's Religions back in 1993. It was, in many ways, a "watershed" event in my life. Going into it, I was a Vice President in a Public Relations firm, who had recently started a side-project of a publishing company, largely to put out my own poetry on a wider scale than the occasional chapbooks I'd self-published over the previous decade or so. At that point I had spent the better part of a decade working with Shamanic teachers, and so gravitated to the neo-Pagan elements in attendance.

The day *after* the Parliament, The Wife and I were taking a little driving vacation, intending to head over by Galena and swing up into south-western Wisconsin to possibly look for some "non-farmable" land to buy for a vacation home. Unfortunately, on the way into Galena, our car started to hydroplane downhill, and we got T-boned by an SUV, landing me in the hospital for months (with pretty much *everything* broken), which ended up as the *coup de grace* for our PR firm, which led me to the decision to jump into the publishing biz full time, using the contacts I'd made at the Parliament to assemble Eschaton's first bunch of authors, landing me in our current state of near-bankruptcy!

Actually, Eschaton's first non-poetry release was a collection of the "Your Voice" newsletters from the Parliament. The PWR was interesting because it was so multi-faceted, there was all the "official" stuff going on (much recounted in this book), but there were all sorts of "community" stuff happening as well, including a newsletter which was published as frequently as three times a day! I have *stories* to tell about that, but they belong in another post, another day.

Anyway ... About A Global Ethic: The Declaration of the Parliament of the World's Religions[2], the book comprises both the "official statement" from the Parliament, and essays by Hans Kung (who was instrumental in writing the Declaration), and Karl-Josef Kuschel, about how this came to be, and the historical context of the Parliament. Frankly, reading the Declaration a dozen years down the pike is a bit of a bittersweet experience ... it's *supposed* to be a statement that all religions could (and pretty much did) subscribe to, but 90% of it would probably cause riots in "the Arab street" these days. It's hard to feel hopeful about a common humanity when a big chunk of that "humanity" is acting like psychotic animals, and isn't much looking to change that any time soon!

I wish that Kuschel would write an update of his "geo-political" analysis of the Parliaments (the first one had been a century previous in 1893, and there have been "regional" ones since), as I feel, at this remove, that those are the most useful parts of the book. Sure, for *me* there were all sorts of things here which were "a trip down memory lane", having been there to experience it ... but it's a way different world in 2006 than it was in 1993, and a lot of what's in the Declaration sounds like it came out of My Little Pony land, and not from any semblance of Reality.

A Global Ethic[3] is still in print, but you can also get it used for a few bucks. I'd recommend it to those who are cynical, or who would like to be. So many things in here are "telling" (like how all the major "evangelical" Christian groups refused to sit down with Buddhists, Hindus, and neo-Pagans, and so boycotted the Parliament), and so many things hint of best intents crushed by Human idiocy.

Ah ... like I said, I have "stories" about this all ... and I'm trying my best to not wander off into them right now.

Notes:

1. http://btripp-books.livejournal.com/11835.html

2-3. http://amzn.to/2bRW1pf

Friday, February 17, 2006[1]

A very silly book ...

O.K., so I should have *guessed* that this was primarily a *humor* book when I picked it up (the cartoons within should have been a give-away, but then again, many of the "new physics" books also use cartoons for illustrating difficult points), but I was, frankly, expecting more of a "psychology/physiology" of napping. This had been "knocking around" since Fathers Day 1997 ... when it was gifted to me by my Father-in-Law ... at that point Daughter #1 was about two and a half years old, and I was past the point of *desperately needing* naps (she had been colicky, and none of us slept much her first six months) so it got put up on the headboard, on the dresser, on a bedroom bookcase, etc. A few weeks ago, Daughter #2 had uncovered it and was waving it at me, and I figured I'd bring it back to my office/library. Looking it over (small format, 96 pages, many illustrations), I figured it would be a quick read, so I tossed it in the "now reading" pile. It actually took me quite a bit longer than I had anticipated, as (no doubt due to the suggestions of the topic) I kept nodding off while trying to read it!

Anyway, as noted above, William A. Anthony's The Art of Napping[2] is a very silly book. He claims to have taken *six years* to write this slim volume, which I guess *must* be a testament of some sort to his expertise with naps. I found his "technical jargon" (nap-*this*ology, nap-*that*ism, etc.) as insufferable as it was inescapable, but there were *some* informational nuggets that were of interest (for instance, the days following Daylight Savings switch-overs have a statistical increase or decrease in *traffic accidents*, 7% more than normal on the days following "losing" an hour and 7% less than normal on the days following "gaining" and hour).

The author of The Art of Napping[3] is a psychology professor at Boston University, and I found myself *deeply hoping* that his various "Nap crusades" pressed in the book were presented with tongue firmly in cheek. Sure, I like napping as much as the next guy, but I'd hate to see Government Departments enforcing "nap breaks" on businesses nationwide! If you really feel a need to read up on napping, this is both still in print, and available via Amazon's new/used for a few bucks. Personally, I don't seek out humor books, so this is "not my thing", but (in the words of Johnny Carson) *"It takes all types to fill the freeway"*, so you might find this to be to *your* liking.

Notes:

1. http://btripp-books.livejournal.com/12092.html
2-3. http://amzn.to/2cudeAT

Sunday, February 19, 2006[1]

A strange little book ...

I picked this up at some bookstore on sale a decade or so back ... probably enticed by the note on the back cover by Shambhala Books' publisher that this was a key inspiration for him getting into publishing. I'm not sure exactly how this text managed that particular spark, but it has elements of "mystery" that could certainly be attractive.

First of all, Rene Daumal's Mount Analogue: A Novel of Symbolically Authentic Non-Euclidean Adventures in Mountain Climbing[2] is *unfinished*, leaving off midsentence in the middle of the fifth chapter of what was to be a seven-chapter work (having been distracted from his writing just prior to his untimely death from tuberculosis at 36, Daumal was never able to complete it). The author[3] had accomplished a remarkable amount in his short life, and was operating in G.I.Gurdjieff's circles (under the wing of Alexadre de Salzmann, to whom the book is dedicated) at the time of his death. The book appears to be an allegory of the mystic path, especially as interpreted by the "4th Way" schools, and, unfortunately, only seems to "get going" in that direction in the unfinished fifth chapter ... giving the reader the sense that they've been handed *half* a map.

On the surface, Mount Analogue[4] is an adventure tale involving the search for a hidden island, with a mountain higher than Everest, which is being sought by an unlikely group of mountaineers. Led by a character who is based on de Salzmann, they chart the location of this and how to approach it through various reasonings (the nature of which does "smell of Gurdjieff"), and set off. Various personal stories and changes are woven into the brief tale, and, no doubt, these would have blossomed as the story continued.

While I found the story interesting (and the biography of Daumal in the introduction *fascinating*), the book *as a book* left me feeling "cheated" ... almost like reading a novel and finding the last half of the book didn't get bound into the cover! Frankly, I would have liked an extensive afterword placing Daumal's works in the context of the Gurdjieffian stream (there appears to be a book[5] from gurdjieff.org which does exactly this), which would, perhaps, hint at the *metaphor* of the subsequent climb/guides/etc.

The Shambhala edition of this is out of print but available used for a few bucks ... there is also a *different* edition in print (in an alternative translation), so it could well be in a bookstore were you interested in finding a copy. I had never encountered Daumal before reading this, so I'm not sure how this really "fits" with his contributions to the art world of the surrealism period, but it is certainly an interesting side-piece to a "4th Way" collection.

Notes:
1. http://btripp-books.livejournal.com/12466.html
2. http://amzn.to/2c7mwVA
3. https://goo.gl/RkXB3Z
4. http://amzn.to/2c7mwVA
5. http://www.gurdjieff.org/rosenblatt1.htm

Tuesday, February 21, 2006[1]

another book ...

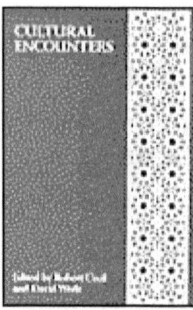

Here's an odd one ... dug out from the nether reaches of my to-be-read shelves, this is a collection of updated papers, whose originals had come out as Institute for Cultural Research monographs, primarily back in the 70's. As noted previously, the ICR was one of Idries Shah's "outreaches", and as such one typically needs to "look beyond the surface" when trying to get a fix on these sorts of books.

Now, Cultural Encounters: Essays on the Interactions of Diverse Cultures Now and in the Past[2], edited by Robert Cecil (ICR Chairman) and David Wade, does not present itself as a "best of" the ICR Monographs (although it is clearly set out that the papers included had all appeared in that series at one point), and in most cases the authors are given opportunity to update and/or expand their texts for this volume. Such a collection would be a bit odd, anyway, as nearly all of the component papers *are still available* in the Monograph format. So, why this book?

Frankly, Cultural Encounters[3] is *highly* uneven in focus and tone ... it is presented in four sections, "Early Eastern Cultures" which has three papers which are primarily historical discussions, "Perceptions of India" which has four papers that range from personal reminiscence to then-current sociology (discussing hippies in various Indian ashrams), "Encounters In The Modern World" which are looks at political development in China, race relations in Columbia, and cultural divisions in Malaysia (quite a mixed bag of sociopolitical issues), and "Global Imperatives" which are typical 1970's "the sky is falling!" looks at ecology, population, and energy with attitudes more like a UN (anti-Western) subcommittee report than anything else. Why this progression? Why re-publish *these* papers?

The book "progresses" from a pre-Western East on through warnings of a "post-Western" dystopian inevitability ... hardly the "Sufi message" that I'm used to seeing in books from Octagon ... except for the final paragraph of the final paper which concludes (in a tone much out of place with the rest of the piece):

> *This alone might give us a little time to get down to the more serious matter of what to do about human nature.*

Now, *that's* a Sufi-esque message, and part of me wonders that the whole book is simply a set-up for that sentence! After all, the book takes a journey from mystery to "golden age" to stress and conflict and ultimately to unsettling future visions ... only to hit the "punch line" that what we *really* need to be working on is human nature!

I had, of course, read all of these papers (in their original forms) previously, so I hit these each with varying degrees of recall. I found it *interesting* that the main "take-away" point that hit my consciousness was one that cropped up in multiple presentations, involving how the Chinese don't "think of religion" the way most other cultures do ... although I can't figure out how *that* factoid would serve a purpose sufficient to make it a "theme" (which it hardly was, but was notable in its coming up in at least *two* of these papers).

I enjoyed reading the first two sections, had some intellectual curiosity about section three, and pretty much had to just grit my teeth and plow through section four. Your mileage may vary ... folks who think that Al Gore is sane and that Michael Moore is worth the space he occupies might have a different take on that. This, like nearly all Octagon books, is still very much in print, but like most Octagon books is very pricey ... $35 for a 260-page book ... though you can get copies though Amazon's new/used vendors for a fourth of that, were this something you felt like pursuing.

Notes:

1. http://btripp-books.livejournal.com/12620.html
2-3. http://amzn.to/2bZ5SWg

Saturday, February 25, 2006[1]

A trip down memory lane ...

Ah, I wonder how long *this* had been on the shelf ... the last time I was down in Mexico was when The Wife was pregnant with Daughter #1, so (given that #1 is ten now), that's got to be at least a decade. I suspect that I picked this up at the remarkable *Museo Nacional de Antropologicia* down in Mexico City (since the first section of this walks you through various areas of the museum). "Back in the day" I used to travel down to Mexico pretty much at least once a year, and did drag The Wife down there a few times before the kids (heck, I *proposed* to her up on top of the Pyramid of the Magician at Uxmal!). Anyway, I probably picked this up on that last trip down there, in '95.

As noted, Archaeological Mexico[2] starts out with a bit of a walk-through of the museum, and then moves out to various sites around Mexico. I figure I'd been to about half of the sites covered (my travels were more in the Yucatan and just around the DF, so I've missed places like Palenque and Monte Alban so far), and it's always cool looking through pictures of places where you've been. Oh, yeah ... I guess it would be good to mention that this is *primarily* a "photo essay" ... each new site gets a few paragraphs of "context" and then there's a paragraph for each picture, but it's heavy on the images ... frankly, by the end, it sort of feels like you've been watching a well-traveled lecturer's vacation snaps rather than "reading a book".

However, if Archaeological Mexico[3] is light on historical details, it does have quite nice photography, and would serve well as an introduction to these sites. I would have appreciated a site map for each to put the various buildings in perspective, but I'm a map freak and "your mileage may vary". Again, if you're *familiar* with the various ruin sites, it's a fun "walk down memory lane", or, if you're not, it's a decent way to know the difference between Chichen Itza and Coba, so I'd say "go for it" ... it's available via Amazon's new/used service both as new (not from Amazon, but via one of their affiliate vendors, at twenty bucks) or as "like new" (unread but with Peso price stickers on the back cover) for under three bucks ... not shabby for a near-coffeetable photo book!

Notes:

1. http://btripp-books.livejournal.com/12978.html
2. http://amzn.to/2bRSaID

Wednesday, March 1, 2006[1]

Another book ...

I haven't gone through one of these National Geographic Society books in a while, and I must admit, they are a *treat*, both for the quality of the photography and the "no B.S." writing style ... add to that a groovy map, and what's not to like?

While not exactly an in-depth (most chapters had 3-4 pages of "over-view" text then "highlights" for various things being discussed) survey, the Stuarts' (a father-and-son writing team) Lost Kingdoms of the Maya[2] is quite a charming historical narrative of the Mayan people, from the earliest emergence to current cultures in Guatamala, Belize, and the Yucatan.

The downside to this early-90's edition is that the National Geographic Society didn't seem to feel that they needed to put an ISBN on it, and I've seen *versions* of this listing some pretty funky publishing entities (from "American Society of Civil Engineers" to MapQuest!), plus the waters seem to be muddied with a video presentation of the same name that came out some time later ... but, hey, that's between me and LibraryThing[3], and shouldn't bother my intrepid readers in the least.

Anyway, this is a nice big coffee-table book (9.5x11") with lots of pretty pictures of very cool ruin sites and archaeological bric-a-brak from them, etc., which is well worth reading for an over-view of the Mayan culture. And, lucky you, there are copies for *under a buck* via Amazon's new/used vendors ... such a deal! This cost $35.00 new, and with shipping you could have it for under $5.00 (and one of the vendors even still has the groovy National Geographic map with it!) ... I'd be all over that deal if, well, I didn't obviously already have the book.

Notes:

1. http://btripp-books.livejournal.com/13182.html
2. http://amzn.to/2bQcc3F
3. http://www.librarything.com/catalog/BTRIPP

Saturday, March 11, 2006[1]

Hey, I did get something read these past few weeks!

Well, while I *have* been largely otherwise occupied these past few weeks, I didn't totally abandon my reading ... in fact about half the sleep I got had this book flopped over on my chest. I'm hoping that things will get more linear in the next week!

The above "sleep" comment is *not* to suggest that A.T. Mann's Sacred Architecture[2] is a snoozefest, because it really isn't ... in fact, it's *quite interesting*, if in an odd disjointed way. I, frankly, had hoped this book was going to be something of a *manual* for Sacred Architecture ... a nuts-and-bolts sort of book that was going to tax my faculties (because, honestly, I don't "get" a lot of the "symbolic geometries" stuff) but leave me enlightened on the subject. I mean, I've read stuff about "The Golden Mean" for decades without getting a sense of what it *means* (if you excuse my pun-like sentence structure). To Mann's credit, I could now (following his diagrams) *illustrate* the concept should, for example, my 10-year-old daughter encounter the term and ask me what it was. However, I *still* would be stumped were she to ask me "why is it special?" or "what is it good for?", and the same is certainly true for the "Vesica Piscis" that he seems to see in everything.

The book does *start* promisingly, as he explains that he was a young architect who kept *waiting* for the time when "the ancient secrets" would be revealed to him, only to find in a post-Bauhaus world, there *were* no architects who thought about that stuff (even if a few might be privy to the information). Unfortunately, he, too, seems to be only willing to skirt the issue ... he did give the subject a name, *"The Canon"*, and provided at least one footnote to a source (remarkably, still in print) ... and spends most of the book drawing those inescapable *newage* diagrams where one takes a map or a building plan and starts sketching out squares, circles, triangles, pentagrams, etc. over it in an effort to "prove something", with neither the "something" nor the "proof" very evident at the end.

On the plus side, the book has a lot of pretty pictures to look at as he covers temples, "the sacred", feng shui, "earth magic", mandalas, and the sacred architecture of Egypt, Islam, and Medieval Europe. He then veers off into a thing about "memory theater" in which he seems to try to link ancient Greek dramatics with Shakespeare, and various Hermeticists, Rosicrucians, and Kabbalists along the way.

Now, this all builds up to the last chapter which is *fascinating*, and could have well be spun off into *two* books. The first of these would be the less interesting, focusing on his hissy-fit about modern architecture, contrasted by only (it would appear) the works of Steiner and Wright; the second would be a very interesting look at "Type I" and "Type II" religions, in which he posits the "downfall" from the former to the latter being in the abandonment of Astrology. Frankly, I think he misses the boat here (or perhaps leaves the unstated hanging in the air), and rather than *blame* the rise of science and rationalism for the ossification of the "Type II" religions, he should be suggesting that it is time for a "Type III" religion/worldview, one that both embraces logic and reason but has room for the intuitive, and the mysterious.

Anyway, despite its frustrating points, Sacred Architecture[3] is quite an interesting read, and if you're given to understanding what's meant when folks start drawing lines all over floorplans, I'm sure you'd get quite a lot out of it! Like most of my current reading list, this has been out for a while, and does not seem to have a current version in print, but through the magic of Amazon's new/used vendor program, a "new" copy can be had for a couple of bucks. And, come on, a book like this has *got* to be a better use for the price of a Mac, soda, and fries.

Notes:

1. http://btripp-books.livejournal.com/13426.html
2. http://amzn.to/2c0yVaE

Tuesday, March 14, 2006[1]

Another one bites the dust ...

As readers of this space who have been paying way too much attention and/or taking notes will no doubt recall, I typically will "juggle" 2-3 books at a time ... in terms of things finding their way to my "read" bookshelves, this ideally provides a constant stream of completed books, although from time to time it means that there will be a flurry of reviews after a long gap. This week appears to be one of the latter cases, and since I'm just starting two new (fairly lengthy) books, it may be another big gap (unless one of the new ones reads faster than it looks going in) before the next set.

Anyway, following up on Sacred Architecture[2] is another "similar" book that I was pretty much reading concurrently, David Fontana's The Secret Language of Symbols : A Visual Key to Symbols and Their Meanings[3]. Frankly, I did not have high expectations for this book, as it had all the "newage" cues of being the equivalent of a "decipher your dreams" sort of book. I was, however, quite surprised at the breadth it achieved, if not the depth (which could hardly be more than it is, given the number of subjects covered in under 200 pages with tons of illustrations).

As I've noted in other posts, I frequently find that I'm the *only person* to have various books in my LibraryThing catalog[4] and I was a bit surprised to find that this was owned by quite a few people over there. I think that is a tribute to The Secret Language of Symbols[5] being quite a nice little over-view of its subject. It has a very logical structure, moving from discussing symbolism in terms of its effects and usage to the main part of the books which is a look at symbols in nearly 50 different categories. The book then closes with a look at various symbol systems, ranging from alchemical symbology to that of the I-Ching. Again, none of these subjects are dwelt on with a great deal of detail, but the book does weave a vast lot of *things* into a rather coherent structure.

One thing I found fascinating was the proposition that the "minor arcana" of the Tarot (what evolved into the standard playing cards of today) originated with teaching images from India, with the various suits having their roots in the "weapons of Vishnu" which represented the different "paths to the divine" (Karma, Bhakti, Gnana, and Raja Yogas) symbolized by the disc, lotus, club, and conch. Here too, this is only sketched out, but there are all sorts of interesting tidbits like this strewn throughout the book, all begging for further reading.

Over-all, I think this would be a very useful book for almost anybody to have ... for those familiar with the subject, it offers gems like this, and to folks who haven't looked at these sort of things it provides a very handy exposition of many different sorts of symbols and systems. Unlike many of the books I've been going through, this one is still in print, and so would be available in a store near you (although Amazon has it at 35% off of cover, and has used copies at under five bucks). Aside from being a useful *reference* it's also a "picture book" featuring hundreds of illustrations ... so I'd think it would be an appealing addition to anyone's library.

Notes:

1. http://btripp-books.livejournal.com/13673.html
2. http://btripp-books.livejournal.com/13426.html
3. http://amzn.to/2bMIvC1
4. http://www.librarything.com/catalog/BTRIPP
5. http://amzn.to/2bMIvC1

Tuesday, March 21, 2006[1]

An interesting read ...

Now, *here's* a rarity ... a book that I just bought! This was actually a "throw in" on an Amazon order I was placing (getting an architecture book to help Daughter #1 with a report she was doing on Mies van der Rohe) ... that book came to just over twenty bucks, and I was poking around in Amazon's sale area to find something that would just nudge the total over $25 to get free shipping. Well, this looked interesting and was just $5.99 on sale. When I was looking for something to follow up that Symbol book in the reading queue, I noticed this sitting out, figured "what the heck?" and jumped into it.

Now, this is a Llewellyn book ... and a *discontinued* Llewellyn book at that. Back when I was in the "metaphysical publishing biz" it was an industry "joke" to see what *whoppers* came out from time to time from "the big L", because, frankly, a *lot* of their titles are pure hoo-hah, but hoo-hah that clueless newagers and witchling wannabes are all too happy to snap up as "ancient wisdom". Given this, I was ready to totally dismiss Richard Herne's (named for the Celtic horned god?) Magick, Shamanism & Taoism: The I Ching in Ritual and Meditation[2], after all, it sounded exactly like the mishmash of assorted mystical stuff that rightfully makes a lot of folks snicker about their releases.

I was, however, quite pleased to find that the first half or so of the book was a very cogent look at the Chinese shamanistic "Wu" tradition, its history, its place in the various Chinese dynasties, its relationship to Tibetan "Bon" practices, how it ended up influencing Taoism, and how Taoism interrelates with traditions such as Japanese Shinto. It then walks the reader through what appear to be adaptations of traditional Chinese exercises and rituals, giving suggestions on how to bring these effectively into a modern, Western context. I always like it when, reading one of these books, I hit something that is "new" to me ... either in a "Wow, I didn't know *that*!" sense or a "What a cool idea!" way. This had one of the latter, with Herne suggesting that, in workings that require one to keep a talisman/sigil on one's person for an extended stretch of time, rather than making it on a bit of paper that would have to be kept track of, drawing it on one's skin with a Mendhi kit! While not being *permanent*, this would allow one to have the symbol always present for an extended period. As they say in the Guinness ads: *Brilliant!*

Most of the second half of the book is taken up with a walk-through of the 64 I-Ching hexagrams. The "purpose" of the book is for meditations on these, so there is a lot of stuff listed for each ... it shows the "Archaic Form" of the corresponding name calligraphy (why?), the "Modern Name" (like the difference between Peking and Beijing), "Esoteric Interpretations", "Opposite Hexagram", "Polarity", "Trigram Combination", "Compass Directions",

"Guardian of the Quarter", "Family Member", "Parts of the Body", "Colors", "Symbolic Creatures", "Plants and Perfumes", "Metals", "Precious Stones", "Emblems", "Ritual Tools", "Gods", "Goddesses", and "Magickal Workings". Confusingly, many of these attributes differ in particular depending on if it's the older "Fu-his" system, or the later "King Wen", but both are given (for example, the compass direction of Hexagram 1 - Ch'ien (Qian) - Heaven is "South"" in Fu-hsi and "Northwest" in King Wen!). Needless to say, if one is *not* particularly looking for bulking up the info for one's I-Ching divinations, this is all "tech manual" stuff, and not particularly gripping reading.

To his credit, Herne closes out Magick, Shamanism & Taoism[3] with some rather informative appendixes, discussing the Taoist Immortals (and their signature symbols), a very interesting list of well over 100 Chinese deities and semi-divine figures, a nice glossary of terms referenced, and assorted other bits of info. If you have an interest in taking a look at Chinese mystical practices, this would be a pretty good place to start ... and since you can get it for as little as $2.50 *new* (through Amazon's new/used vendors), it's a pretty good deal.

Notes:

1. http://btripp-books.livejournal.com/13915.html

2-3. http://amzn.to/2c4AAiC

Sunday, March 26, 2006[1]

Another book ...

This was an odd one ... I still am not sure *why* the book was set up the way it was. Brian M. Fagan's Kingdoms of Gold, Kingdoms of Jade: The Americas Before Columbus[2] starts with the contact-era cultures of the Aztecs and the Incas, but then jumps back to theories of initial native settlement in North America, discussing Hunting societies, Fishing societies, and Farming societies, their development, etc. (and geographically ranging all over the place in the process). The book then goes into an Olmec - Mayan - Mayan/Toltec section, and then sort of backtracking to "pre-Aztec" cultures (Teotihuacan/Toltec), jumping back down to South America to deal with the pre-Incan cultures of the Chavin, Moche, and various other regional groups, and then moving north again to look at North America in only the context of the Pueblo cultures and the Mississippian/Moundbuilders. Obviously, the author wanted to "anchor" the book on the period of European contact, and then explore what came before ... but it really did seem to lack a certain sense of "structure".

This is not to say that any of the individual bits of Kingdoms of Gold, Kingdoms of Jade[3] are badly done. Section-by-section the book is quite interesting, and lavishly illustrated with plates ranging from Catherwood lithos to museum items, to aerial shots of ruin sites, to "anthropological" portraits, to reproductions from assorted codexes and pottery, to plan diagrams of sites (some, like Chavin de Huantar, I'd not seen in that detail previously) done specifically for this volume, etc., etc., etc.

Interestingly (to me, at least), I can't find anything on-line about this *paperback* edition ... everything seems to point to the hardcover version (and this, being from 1991, just on the edge of universal ISBN use, managed to get into print without one in or on the book, so there might be a different record out there for the paperback, I just can't find it!). Why should you care? Well, if you're interested in picking up a copy, all the links I have go to the hardcover ... now, admittedly, this seems to be out of print at this point, and you *can* get a used copy via Amazon's new/used vendor service for as little as 86¢ ... but it bugs me to not be able to refer to *this* edition!

Any caveats? Well ... aside from the strange (and/or lack of) structure ... the author takes a couple (and just 2 or 3, this isn't like that *Dreamtime* book with Luddite rants) shots at "modern western culture" of the environmental Chicken Little variety, which should have been bitch-slapped out of the book by his editors. That sort of stuff always seems like the writer is trying to prove how *progressive* or *aware* or *hip* he/she is when it's gratuitously dropped into a book like this! I also have some questions about some of the figures he uses in here about disease patterns in North America, especially in light of the *other* book I'm currently reading, *Native American History* which paints the Native depopulation (especially in the Eastern states) as more a matter of "ethnic cleansing" than frontiersmen finding "empty villages" on their way west.

Having read a great deal in this particular area, I have some pretty solid opinions on the topic, and while I don't much care for how Fagan tries to "weave together" all these cultures (he sort of tries to suggest a common "jaguar" motif, which while obvious in several cultures, is something of a "reach" in others) he presents a decent picture of each on its own, and adds in interesting details that I hadn't previously encountered. Since you can get a copy for cheap, you might consider picking this up (if for just the pictures).

Notes:

1. http://btripp-books.livejournal.com/14280.html
2-3. http://amzn.to/2c0xUQb

Saturday, March 30, 2006[1]

One last one for March ...

Did you ever have a professor who just rubbed you the wrong way? Somebody who, while they may have known their shit and was an effective teacher, just constantly made you want to bitchslap them? That was the vibe I was getting from the author of the current book.

The New Archaeology and the Ancient Maya[2] is really more about Jeremy A. Sabloff's views about "The New Archaeology" than the Maya. Sure, the book *discusses* the Maya (they *are*, after all, the subject of his fieldwork), but I got the feeling that the Maya were just the *excuse* for pushing Sabloff's style of archaeological research in this book. He reminds me of the MBAs spewing out of the business schools back in the 80's, hellbent to implement their new models and not interested in what had proven effective before they arrived on the scene.

This is not to say that the book is without value, it provides an interesting comparison between "old archaeology", which concentrated almost exclusively on the "major works" of a culture (or, as the author puts it "of the *Elite*"), versus the supposed "new archaeology" which seems more like anthropological forensics operating within a context that has more than whiff of tacit Marxist paradigms. Again, I am reminded of many an argument in college with Leftist friends about what constituted "culture" and how the tangible arts helped define that. Now, it's not that Sabloff is explicitly saying that the pyramids and palaces *don't matter*, but he seems more interested in the stuff that fell between the cracks in peasant hovels.

Thanks, no doubt, to this being part of the Scientific American Library, the book *is* beautifully illustrated, especially with a collection of really remarkable photos (many shot just on the edge of storms, most with amazing skies) which give a fresh perspective to many familiar ruins! I was also amused to find in one photo what would appear to be the "source" of the "Jungle Ruin" hole[3] in Sierra's classic *3-D Ultra Minigolf* game ... a side temple off of the main plaza at Tikal!

Anyway, this isn't a *bad* book, just *preachy* (or maybe it's just pushing *my* buttons) ... but with lots of interesting bits and pieces and pretty pictures to look at. If you didn't know much about the Maya, I wouldn't recommend starting off with this one, but if you've built up some *context* in which to place Sabloff's theories, it's a decent addition to your library. And, hey ... Amazon's new/used vendors have a "very good" copy for 50¢ ... the photography alone is worth that (plus the $3.49 shipping).

Notes:
1. http://btripp-books.livejournal.com/14427.html
2. http://amzn.to/2cqIocD
3. https://goo.gl/8VZHME

Saturday, April 1, 2006[1]

Sorta taking a break ...

OK, so every now and again I get "overloaded" on a particular theme ... and while I still have a couple of nice thick books on the subject beckoning me from my to-be-read shelves, I really had to take a break from the Mayan/archaeology books that I've been plowing through of late. What I needed was some "fluff", and I figured a book or two on Angels might just be the thing! Actually, this book (and its follow-up, which I started this evening) "suggested themselves" more on *format* than subject ... these have been "flopping" out of stacks of other unread books due to their approximately 8x8" size, and as the most recent Mayan book (a hardcover) was also nearly square, I figured that it would "work on the shelf" to get to these at this point.

Now, if *that's* not a glowing recommendation, I don't know what would be (hah!). Actually, I was *surprised* that Sophy Burnham's A Book of Angels[2] wasn't a total newage fluff-fest. Frankly, the first 2/3rds of the book are a quite interesting, the first section dealing with the author's interface with metaphysical realities and the second section being a decent survey on the history of "angels" both in varied cultural settings and how the concept has developed in the Judeo-Christian tradition (most of what the majority of people would recognize as "angel lore" comes from fictional, rather than scriptural, contexts, Dante's The Divine Comedy[3] and Milton's Paradise Lost[4] specifically, to the extent that the "Shavian Satan" says of the latter, in Shaw's Man And Superman[5], *"and to this day every Briton believes that the whole of his silly story is in the Bible"*!).

The *last third* of the book, however, *does* take a turn towards "newage sewage" (why Burnham decides that she has to go into what I'd consider "overshare", I don't know, but I guess that plays better with "the angel market" than it does to me) with her unburdening herself of various *stuff*, and then a section of letters that folks sent in to her when word got out that she was working on this book project. Of course, if that's "your thing" you might have a different opinion ... considering the book I just started into is nothing *but* more of these letters, I'm sure that's going to be a swell read (heck, it probably won't be any goofier than Weird Illinois[6] was).

Anyway, this was not a *bad* read ... it was certainly a whole lot more tolerable than I had anticipated when I decided to start reading it, and it *does* have some very interesting bits in the middle section, with an over-all impression which puts the book in the category that Arsenio Hall used to frame as *"things that make you go hmmmm ..."*, which is OK by me. And ... should you care to check it out ... A Book of Angels[7] can be had used via the Amazon new/used vendors for as little as a penny ... and a *new* copy (from the same source) can be had for as little as 40¢ ... such a deal!

Notes:
1. http://btripp-books.livejournal.com/14706.html
2. http://amzn.to/2cqHufY
3. http://amzn.to/2c4ypLI
4. http://amzn.to/2bPajae
5. http://amzn.to/2cqHrRf
6. http://btripp-books.livejournal.com/1555.html
7. http://amzn.to/2cqHufY

Sunday, April 2, 2006[1]

Yuck ...

Ew ... ew ... ew .. ew ... *EW!*

At least it was *short*. Everything that I'd feared that A Book of Angels[2] was going to be, this one was, and then some! Why does this book exist? The publisher's quote on Amazon says this is a "perennial holiday favorite" which is just plain *depressing*. It's like all the "good" letters went into the first book, but they still were coming in and the publisher decided this was a way to cash in cheap. Bleh.

As you would guess, Sophy Burnham's Angel Letters[3] are letters that folks have sent in to her in response to reading its predecessor. It doesn't have much of a real structure, but Burnham occasionally interjects some commentary to preface a grouping. And, frankly, there are not that many "Angels" in this book, with about the first 2/3rds being stuff like:

> *"So there ah was, just finished eatin' and ah couldn't find the top ta mah ketchup bottle ... ah knew that if ah didn't cap it, mah ketchup would get all gummy and nasty, so ah looked every which where fo it ... but it was jus' GAWN! ... ah hated ta think ah'd have ta git me a new bottle, so ah prayed ta JEEEEESUS ta help me in mah hour of need ... ah went down on mah knees right there in the dinin' nook and when ah gots up, there it was! ... right in front of mah eyes! ... it shorely was a miracle! ... ah feel so touched by da LAWD!"*

I mean, the sort of "common people being clueless" stories that I can recall from Readers Digest (and, needless to say, the above quote is my *mockery* of these and not an actual excerpt from the book). The last 1/3 of the book was not much better but it primarily shifted from *Jeeeeesus* to newagey feelgood twaddle ("I never felt so close to the universe before!").

Frankly, there were *maybe* three stories in here which provided *any* help for "understanding Angels" (and one of those would be better classified as a story about *ghosts*), but as noted in regards to the previous book, "your mileage may vary" ... as if you want to hear "I must have been helped by God because that sort of thing doesn't happen naturally", despite there being assorted more mundane explanations, have at it!

One thing I find either amusing or sad is that the publisher for these books is Ballantine Books, the source for the magnificent military/political history books from the '60s and '70s published as "Ballantine's Illustrated History of the Violent Century", of which I have 48 volumes in my LibraryThing catalog[4]! It's a long fall from the excellence of those books to the sort of drivel in Angel Letters[5].

However, if you *want* this sort of thing, you can have it for *cheap*, as the Amazon new/used vendors have copies of the *hardcover* edition for as little as one cent. I guess this is still in print in paperback, but this ain't worth the $3.49 to pay for shipping, let alone fifteen bucks for it new.

Notes:

1. http://btripp-books.livejournal.com/14998.html
2. http://btripp-books.livejournal.com/14706.html
3. http://amzn.to/2c0vQaB
4. http://btripp-books.com
5. http://amzn.to/2c0vQaB

Monday, April 3, 2006[1]

That's more like it ...

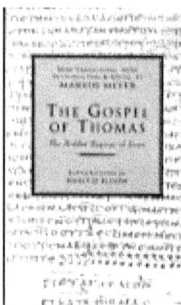

So, I needed *something* to get the ickiness of Angel Letters[2] out of my head, but I wasn't *quite* ready to shift genres. Poking around on the "to be read" shelves, I found this slim volume of Serious Reading, and figured that it would just about do the trick!

Frankly, I should have *probably* read this one back when I was doing a lot of Dead Sea Scrolls reading (although the source material here was from the Nag Hammadi finds) ... especially in light of the formatting, with the Coptic originals presented across from their English translations. Actually, if I had a quibble with Marvin Meyer's The Gospel of Thomas: The Hidden Sayings of Jesus[3], it would be in the format of the second and third sections, as in the second section the texts are presented across from the translations, but then you need to skip ahead fifty pages to the analysis of each of the 114 apothegms that comprise the text. I would have found it more useful/natural to have the Coptic text, the English translation and the notes thereto all in a column for each, progressing through the work that way ... but, again, that's just a quibble from somebody who used to get to design books.

While Meyer provides an interesting introduction placing The Gospel of Thomas[4] within its historical, linguistic, and theological contexts, it's Harold Bloom's "interpretation" section that really makes this book a delight. Aside from asking the "elephant in the living room" question (which I'm paraphrasing here) of *"if Jesus spoke Aramaic to his followers, how good a translation do we have in texts that were written in Greek a generation or more after the fact?"*. It is argued that the sayings *quoted* in Thomas are far closer to the actual teachings of whoever this Jesus person was than anything that later got cobbled together into the Bible!

If you look at the reviews on Amazon, the Biblical Literalists have the torches and pitchforks out for this book ... and I have come to expect that if a Bible Thumper is busting a blood vessel over something, that something probably has more Truth in it than the Thumper's favorite book.

Speaking of Amazon ... you can, oddly enough, get a *new* hardcover (remaindered) copy for a lot less than a used paperback (which is still in print) ... a couple of these are going for under $3.00, not bad for a $19.95 list price book. This is one that I'd definitely recommend to anybody with an interest in religious texts (or generally irritating the Fundies!).

P.S. -

I don't typically like to add on *rants* to these little reviews, but I was *aghast* to find out how a book that Bloom highly recommends, Burton Mack's *A Myth of Innocence: Mark and Christian Origins*, has been driven out of the market. Mack's book is one that takes that "Aramaic question" and runs it out to a very logical conclusion ... that Jesus didn't *found* Christianity, but that "Christians", decades after Jesus's death, *invented* the story of his life, ministry, divinity, etc., etc., etc., to support their cult (once it became clear that the initial assumption that Jesus was "coming back any day now" was off the mark). I'm assuming that this book has been *systematically* "disappeared" (much like John Allegro's remarkable *The Sacred Mushroom and the Cross*) by Christians trying to erase the "uncomfortable questions"! Mack's book had a list price of $26.00 (for about 440 pages) but it will cost you at least *twice* that to get a *used* copy, and some vendors are charging as much as *four hundred bucks* to get one! The only plausible excuse for this sort of "rarity" is that Xtian Fundamentalists are destroying any copies they can lay their hands on ... which I suppose IS a lot easier than having to *face the questions* that these books raise about their religion!

Notes:

1. http://btripp-books.livejournal.com/15296.html
2. http://btripp-books.livejournal.com/14998.html
3-4. http://amzn.to/2bP8KsE

Thursday, April 6, 2006[1]

Wow ...

This is an *amazing* book! I thought that I was fairly conversant with the details of American History (being a Mayflower Descendant on 2 lines and all), but this was a HUGE eye-opener. I mean, I knew that the Indians had been *screwed* by the Government, but I never suspected how across-the-board the bad faith dealings had been, and how *intentional* it all seems to have been. As "my people" have been over here for the better part of the past 400 years, I'm looking at all sorts of ugly Karma outlined in this book ... being of "northern" stock, I've always felt like I could take a pass on "slavery guilt", but it's hard to duck what was done to the Eastern Tribes.

Frankly, I feel that Judith Nies' Native American History: A Chronology of a Culture's Vast Achievements and Their Links to World Events[2] should be featured in every high school's History curriculum. When people act surprised about our government doing "ugly things" they're usually basing that surprise on the sugar-coated cartoon version of our history that we get fed in school ... I was *amazed* at the prevalence of *pure evil* (usually dressed up as Christianity "saving" those Heathen Savages) that was the RULE rather than the exception during our entire time on this continent. Even figures like Thomas Jefferson (himself no great fan of Christianity) is shown in this book as *deliberately* double-crossing various tribes in the interest of land acquisitions for the fledgling USA. ... very disturbing stuff.

The book is set up in an unusual format, with a column of "World History" on one half of each page and a column of "Native American History" on the other, with chapters going from 28,000bc to 1bc, 1ad to 1400ad, and a chapter each for the centuries following. The text walks the reader through the years, and it's interesting to see how events in Europe and elsewhere intertwined with things happening here. There are also "mini-chapters" on key figures and happening inserted at various points in the book, and a number of maps. Some of these maps are quite damning, where they show the wide distribution of native tribes on areas that our "official history" paints as "virgin land". Of course, in the early decades following European contact, the diseases brought across the Atlantic did most of the damage, with many cultures losing as much as 90% of their populations, leaving the weakened survivors easy prey for the encroaching White Man (uh, that would be my folks).

Needless to say, I *highly* recommend that you pick up a copy of Native American History[3] ... I think it's something that *every* American should read to place the perversity of the Federal Government in its proper context! Amazon has this at a very reasonable $9.75 *new* (although there is one used copy available for as little as $2.25), marked down from its $15.00 cover price. However, I think this one is important enough for people to check out, that paying cover at a bookstore is well worth it!

Notes:
1. http://btripp-books.livejournal.com/15508.html
2-3. http://amzn.to/2c6KaDb

Thursday, April 13, 2006[1]

Three small books ...

While down in Phoenix this past weekend, I got in one activity that I (as opposed to the kids or the in-laws) wanted to do, which was go visit the Pueblo Grande[2] archaeological site. This is pretty remarkable, being right downtown, just east of the airport. Of course, the whole greater Phoenix area had been home to the Hohokam a thousand years ago, so finding their remains is not unusual in that regards. The Pueblo Grande site has a large mound with various associated additional buildings (and several more acres not fully excavated), with a small museum attached. I picked up these three guidebooks in the museum gift shop.

As those reading these posts regularly know, I used to have a small publishing company, and I'm quite envious that the publisher of these has been able to "make a go of it" with these quarter-page format saddle-stitched books. I was also impressed that these were the first books I've seen that featured the new "ISBN-13" identification numbering (also indicating to me that these are in enough demand for frequent re-printing). As these are quite brief (32 pages each), I figured I'd cover them all in one review.

First, there is Elizabeth C. Welsh's Easy Field Guide to Southwestern Petroglyphs[3], a decent over-view of what petroglyphs are, how they were (variously) made, how they can or can't be dated, etc. There are tons of illustrations of assorted petroglyphs, with information about what "style" each is, and some conjecture as to what they might mean. This is an interesting discussion, as it brings in interpretations of current Southwest native tribal experts, as well as examples from our own culture (e.g. would somebody 300 years from now recognize Smokey The Bear as an icon for forest fire awareness?).

Next is James R. Cunkle's Easy Field Guide to Indian Art & Legends of the Southwest[4] which looks at Southwestern native myths as they've "survived" in the pottery of the Mimbres people, part of the Mogollon culture of 1,000 years ago. The Mimbres burial customs involved placing a bowl over the face of the deceased, with a small hole punched through the bottom, and these bowls have been excavated in various locations over the years, and form the basis of this booklet. Thirty three bowls are pictured, with a brief explanation (or conjecture) of what the design represents. Some are easily recognizable (with variations of Kokopelli or Hopi "trickster" figures), while some are interpreted via other known Native American myths, and some are just described, with their significance guessed at. Again, hardly exhaustive (although a more extensive book[5] by the same author is recommended in the intro), it is an interesting way of presenting the subject.

Finally, there's Rick Harris' Easy Field Guide to Rock Art Symbols of the Southwest[6], which is sort of thematically between the other two. This is primarily the description of nearly 200 symbols, ranging from clan icons to spirit and animal imagery, with outlines on how to "read" things like directional cues, and combination symbols (such as "trail leads to settlement beyond mountains"). I'm sure that the Von Danikens of this world will really appreciate the fact that *all* the "Spirits" pictured look exactly like the heads of classic pulp-era SciFi robots (except for the one that looks like that <u>Popping Martian</u>[7] thing!), including what could easily have been the prototype for "Dr. Theopolis" from the cheesy *Buck Rogers in the 25th Century* TV show.

I'd normally point folks off to Amazon to pick up copies of these (were you so inclined), however, Amazon proper, while listing these, has a "sourcing fee" added on that's more than the cost of the ($1.50 list) book, and their used/new vendor area adds on $3.50 shipping per title! So, if you're looking to pick up these, I'd recommend going straight to the publisher, <u>American Traveler Press</u>[8], where you'd just end up spending $2.50 for shipping for all three.

Notes:

1. http://btripp-books.livejournal.com/15840.html
2. https://www.phoenix.gov/parks/arts-culture-history/pueblo-grande
3. http://amzn.to/2bP6T7f
4. http://amzn.to/2cqDbRX
5. http://amzn.to/2c6Ku4l
6. http://amzn.to/2c0u3IP
7. http://amzn.to/2cqEyjo
8. http://americantravelerpress.com/

Sunday, April 16, 2006[1]

What interesting timing ...

I find it somewhat amusing that I finished Kevin Rushby's Children of Kali: Through India in Search of Bandits, the Thug Cult, and the British Raj[2] on *Easter*, as it has some very interesting things to say about Christianity.

Frankly, I sort of ""stumbled onto" this book ... I'm reading another couple at the moment, both of which are progressing at a slower pace that I would have preferred ... however, this past Wednesday Daughter #1 and I had to run downtown to the big B&N on State St. to get a book she was *supposed* to be reading over Spring Break, and which was (predictably) gone from the local library and closer bookstores. When I discovered that *her* book was under six bucks, I decided that I'd "treat myself" to a purchase from B&N's "bargain" section, where I found (the $27.00 cover-price) Children of Kali[3] for a mere $5.98 (such a deal!). It looked interesting enough, and I figured that at under ¾-off it was just *begging* me to pick it up.

I was surprised to find that the book was more of a travelogue than an analysis of the Thugee cult, or of Kali-worship in general. This was, I found, due to the *author's* surprise in his researches in India to find very little data to support the *reality* of there ever having *been* such a cult, or at least a cult of the sort luridly portrayed in the popular literature of the British Raj. Rushby details his journeys around India, the leads he followed, the experts he spoke with, and his readers (in my case at least) feel the growing sense of frustration ... it was almost like he was traveling in some future USA looking for the "real Easter Bunny".

While "Thugs" did (and, perhaps *do*) evidently exist in some form, the savage "kill-for-Kali cult" that is "common knowledge" in the West seems to be a fabrication of the agents of the East India Company and the British Crown, with full support (and possibly initial "conceptualization") by Christian Evangelical groups like the Salvation Army.

Rushby's research points to a scenario that goes a bit like this ... China had been opened up for trade through a series of European military successes ... one of the key things that the British were selling in China was *opium* ... in order to *supply* enough opium for the huge China market, the British decided to switch considerable swaths of agricultural land in India over to poppy production and away from basic food crops ... for many castes and regional cultural groups in India this resulted in areas suffering near starvation, and a general steep decline in living standards ... responding to these *economic* forces, numerous of these castes and cultural groups turned towards banditry. Up until this point there had, while being regions where travel *was hazardous*, never been reports of "cult attacks", however, with the increase of the presence of highwaymen the new officials of the Raj were instructed to "clean it up", and the face they gave it was of a "murder cult" breathlessly fleshed out by Christian missionaries. To the Indians, the "Thugs" were simply con-men and robbers, who *may* have killed in the pursuit of their looting (some looting was better than others, as the opium trade resulted in large amounts of cash criss-crossing the subcontinent via couriers). None of the informants that Rushby interviews could provide *any* traditions of cultic activities associated with this.

Needless to say, this came as a shock to me ... I had anticipated a gripping over-view of a blood-soaked brotherhood of killers, dedicated to the Dark Mother ... and I suspect it disappointed the author as well. This is my main caveat about the book ... it leads the reader off on a "quest" but discovers that *"there's no THERE there"*, so one is left with the search, the impressions, and the realization that we've been lied to again.

Again, finding another "big lie" oozing out of the efforts of Christianity to destroy a native culture is not a huge surprise, but it's somewhat ironic on the timing, being Easter and all.

Anyway, while not being "gripping", Children of Kali[4] was involving enough that I breezed through it in just a handful of days, so you might find it of interest as well. For some reason Amazon has this at full cover, while B&N (in the store I was in, at least) had it for under $6.00 ... you can get this via the Amazon used/new vendors *new* for about $7.00 (plus shipping) ... so your best bet to pick this one up (were you so inclined) would be to check the discount shelves at your local B&N, although getting from the Amazon vendors would still be under half price with shipping.

Notes:

1. http://btripp-books.livejournal.com/16111.html
2-4. http://amzn.to/2cqBYKw

Sunday, April 23, 2006[1]

NOT a quick read this time ...

OK, so here's one of *those books*, an exercise in intellectual calisthenics rather than something "that I wanted to read". Frankly, I'm not sure when this got into my library ... it's old enough that it *could* have been a holdover from college, but it wasn't filed like that (and I don't recall it hanging around that long), but it seemed like something to "get read" at this point, so I plowed through it over the past several weeks. Raymond B. Blakney's Meister Eckhart: A Modern Translation[2] dates to 1941, so "modern" is in the long view. It's amusing that some of the introductory commentary and footnotes make "current event" reference to the Nazis, and how they were using various elements of Germanic Mysticism to support their world-view. Obviously, this version was left as it stood back then (through evidently *many* printings), but you'd think that somebody at some point might have updated some of that stuff.

If you're not familiar with the name, Meister Eckhart was a 13th/14th Century German Dominican cleric, of great intellect, wide study, and personal force. According to Blakney, Eckhart seems to have been familiar with a broad range of spiritual knowledge, from the classic thinkers of ancient Greece, to Lao Tzu in China and the Upanishads in India, and he brought these threads together in his writings and sermons. Unfortunately for him, he tended to "riff" in his sermons, coming up with spontaneous "uncovered truths" which blurred the line of heresy. Also unfortunate was that he came from a region rife with "mystical heresies", and soon became the target of the Franciscans, who eventually succeeded in bringing him before the Inquisition in his 60's, leading to his eventual (although undocumented) demise.

Eckhart's ego certainly did not help in his problems with the Inquisition. The last sections of this book deal with his defense to various charges made against either his written teachings or the reports of his various sermons ... here's a sampling of how he framed his defense: *"[Careful studies of his words] reveal the intellectual weakness or malice of my opponents, rather than their manifest blasphemy or even heresy ..."* Yep, nothing like calling your accusers stupid and evil to grease the skids of justice!

Blakney's Meister Eckhart[3] presents several of his early works, a couple of dozen "sermons", bits and pieces of fragmentary works and "legends" about him, and the text of his 1326 "Defense" against the Inquisition. It provides a very interesting look at a man's vision of the Divine which *strongly* effected many movements that followed.

Amazon's got this at its $15.00 cover price, but you can pick one up for less with their new/used vendors. While I recommend this, I recommend it specifically to those with an interest in Western mysticism and "Church History" (and I was, after all, a Religion Major, so have a background suitable to processing this stuff without too much boredom creeping in). If you're looking at a way of injecting a mystical awareness into a *very* Christian structure (needless to say, I would have much preferred an outright *heretical* version!), this might also be of interest.

Notes:

1. http://btripp-books.livejournal.com/16288.html
2-3. http://amzn.to/2bOQShA

Thursday, April 27, 2006[1]

Interesting ...

I've had this book sitting around since the middle of the Klinton regime (when I was certain those bastards would ban all access to the Constitution ... I figured I needed a copy in my possession), but it didn't suggest itself for the "current read" pile until just recently (perhaps by this[2] was the trigger). Anyway, I figured, what good is a Libertarian if he doesn't have easy access to the Constitution, right?

Well, Harold J. Spaeth's The Constitution of the United States[3] is a bit of a strange duck. One would *think* that a book so titled would, perhaps, concentrate *most* of its verbiage *on the Constitution* ... however, Spaeth's book spends only the first 10% or so discussing it, then devotes the next 70% to looking at how the Supreme Court has interfaced with it over the years (up to 1990, this being the 1991 edition). The actual Constitution itself is buried back in Appendix F, stuck between a couple of editions of The Federalist and the Confederate Constitution!

Frankly, I would have been MUCH more interested in this had the focus been on the materials dumped in the back ... the Virginia Bill of Rights of (1776), the Declaration of Independence (1776), the Articles of Confederation (1781), The Federalist #10 (1787), The Federalist #51 (1788), the U.S. Constitution (1789), and the C.S. Constitution (1861). While he does, *briefly* touch on the antecedents of the Constitution and the fight over Federalism, this would have been a far better book had the thrust been on how the Constitution got to be the way it is, with comparisons to similar documents, rather than a look at what the Supreme Court has done with it. It's almost "false advertising" that there is NO mention of the Supreme Court on the cover, as this is not a book *about* the Constitution, but about how the Court has interpreted it in various cases in assorted "topics" over the years ... a more honest title would have been something like *"The Supreme Court's approach to The Constitution"* or something along those lines

Of course, the fact that Spaeth "wears his Leftism on his sleeve" for most of the book (sneering at Conservative judges/decisions and waxing into breathless enthusiasm for the most radical of the 60's judicial excesses) didn't help my enjoyment of it. I have since discovered that the author is a member of the Michigan Democratic State Central Committee, so his is hardly a neutral voice! On the plus side, it's written for college students, so it's at about the 8th grade reading level ... which made it (up until the documents in the Appendices, of course), a quick and easy read.

Now, I probably *read* the Constitution somewhere back in High School, but the details hardly stayed with me ... what struck me, however, was the economy of words .. I'm not sure if "terseness" or "brevity" fits, but when you have the Second Amendment (in total) say:

> *"A well regulated Militia, being necessary to the security of a free State, the right of the people to keep and bear Arms shall not be infringed."*

It hardly leaves much "wiggle room" ... which makes me wonder what part of "the right of *the people* to *keep and bear Arms*" or *"shall not be infringed"* the anti-gun Leftists can't get! You can't have an effective Militia unless you can assemble *armed citizens*. Of course, the Lefties think everything *comes from the Government* so they try to argue that the Militia is something somehow provided BY the Government, rather than being a safeguard that the People have *against* excesses OF the Government.

Anyway ... I can't much recommend this one ... I'm sure there are better books on the Constitution out there. It is perhaps telling, that while this is still in print (it is, after all, in the HarperCollins College Outline series, so is no doubt being used as a text book), this 13th edition, from 1991, was the last update. If the idea of a Leftist review of Supreme Court decisions sounds yummy to you, it can be had *new* from the usual suspects for as little as a buck seventy five. I'd recommend a cup of coffee instead.

Notes:

1. http://btripp-books.livejournal.com/16420.html
2. http://btripp-books.livejournal.com/15508.html
3. http://amzn.to/2bOPtYn

Wednesday, May 3, 2006[1]

an odd read ...

OK ... so, the key word in the title of Barry Raftery's Pagan Celtic Ireland: The Enigma of the Irish Iron Age[2] is "*Enigma*", or that at least was *my* "take away" on the book. Much like another book[3] I recently read, there is a real sense of "there being no *there* there", although in this case there obviously *was* an Iron Age in Ireland, and it involved people who were, it would certainly seem, *Celtic*, it's just that ... well, there's not much *evidence*.

I guess that one of the problems of living in a cold, wet climate (as opposed to a hot, dry climate ala Egypt or much of Mexico), is that it's hard to leave behind a lot of stuff, especially if that stuff tends to decompose. One of the things that really struck me in this book (but which I, unfortunately, neglected to jot down the specific details of) was just how scanty some remains were ... five of this thing, fifteen of that, for *all of Ireland*. Almost all of what the archaeologists can point to are things deliberately dumped in some ritual context (in rivers, lakes, bogs, etc.) ... that would be almost like having no record of the Maya except for what was dredged out of the sacred Cenote at Chichen Itza! It also didn't help much that most of the "elite" (i.e., those who would be likely to have notable "grave goods") seemed to have been cremated rather than interred, meaning that there was a LOT less "stuff" to start with.

The book looks at *major* undertakings like the Hillforts, and the Corlea roadway, and notes that there is NO data on where the people who actually built these things lived. Even the major sites show only sporadic signs of being occupied. Much of what is attributed to the Irish in this period is based on other "Celtic" cultures, in Northern Europe (the "Hallstatt Culture" in Austria or the "La Tène Culture" in Switzerland), appearing in traces across the northern half of Ireland, with other influences (Iberian Celtic culture) showing up in the great fortifications in the southern half.

Given these caveats, Pagan Celtic Ireland[4] is interesting enough, discussing what materials there are in detail, with a lot of helpful illustrations and photos. It is structured on major topics (political structure, technology and art, ritual and death, etc.) and looks at what *can be* said about these based on the actual surviving archaeological traces. Perhaps this is where the author stumbles ... were he to "riff" off of "what is *known*" and into speculation, it would have been a more vibrant read ... but limiting the "story line" to what could be defended by the minimal actual evidence kept things to a slow shuffle. Unfortunately, if you wanted to get a copy of this you're going to have to shell out about twenty bucks, either for the paperback via Amazon, or the hardcover *used*. Frankly, I'd recommend borrowing this one from the library first before spending the money.

Notes:
1. http://btripp-books.livejournal.com/16679.html
2. http://amzn.to/2bUtPwv
3. http://btripp-books.livejournal.com/16111.html
4. http://amzn.to/2bUtPwv

Thursday, May 4, 2006[1]

Much better ...

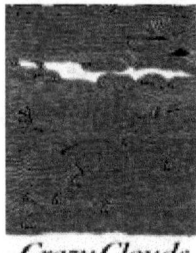

Ah, look, books falling like flies! Actually, I would have been done with this one several days ago, but I put it aside to push through the Irish book for "*shelf*ish reasons" (i.e. how books of various sizes and formats would line up). So this one showing up here so "close on the heels" of the previous review was just a "book juggling" quirk.

I'm happy to report that Perle Besserman & Manfred Steger's book, Crazy Clouds: Zen Radicals, Rebels & Reformers[3] was a *delight* to read. Engagingly written, informative, and not (well, except for a tiny bit in the Epilogue) preachy, it provides a very useful window to its subject, that being various Zen teachers over the years.

I really liked the *structure* of this book. It moves, chapter by chapter, from the 8th century on up to the present day (well, the late 1980's at least), with each chapter focusing on one Zen teacher, and each chapter having more or less the same internal format ... a bit of history of the politics and religion of the era, a bio on the individual Zen master, and a discussion on his particular style of teaching and how it interfaced with the secular world and the religious tradition. This is subtly presented (i.e., the chapters aren't broken up into sections like this), but almost gives a sense that the book could have been a series of pamphlets on the eight teachers covered. These are, in order: P'ang Yun, Rinzai, Bassui, Ikkyu, Bankei, Hakuin, Nyogen Senzaki, and Soen. The last on this list, Nakagawa Soen Roshi, was known to Ms. Besserman (it's not clear if she was a *student* or not, or had simply spent time at one of his retreat centers), prior to his death in 1984.

I must admit that, while I have *read* a lot of Zen material over the years, I have never been able to make myself sit zazen. Even exposure to Richard Baker Roshi on various journeys (Richard is a good friend of one of my Shamanic teachers, and came along on some adventures I had in my 30's) was unable to get me over that "can't sit" thing. I do, however, really appreciate the cognitive aspects of Zen (if clouded by my busy mind), and it's always a treat to come across a book like this that lets me get in touch with some of this.

Again, Crazy Clouds[3] is a collection of stories about the *people* who made Zen what it is, not a collection of the *teachings* (although there are certainly elements of those that shine through), so it's much more accessible than a book that is meant for Zen *study*, and I very highly recommend it. This is, understandably, still in print, so you should be able to find it locally (for $13), but you can get it used for less through Amazon, etc. If you have *any* interest in Zen, this is a book that you will appreciate having in your library!

Notes:

1. http://btripp-books.livejournal.com/16956.html
2-3. http://amzn.to/2bMGiHU

Sunday, May 7, 2006[1]

A fascinating little book ...

Sometimes I "stumble over things" on-line and see a reference and think *"hey, I have that!"*, and this was one of those cases. I'd recently had a "men's workshop" recommended to me and was doing some background research on it, and saw Robert Moore & Douglas Gillette's King, Warrior, Magician, Lover: Rediscovering the Archetypes of the Mature Masculine[2] listed as one of the "mythopoetic" sourcebooks that they use. I really don't recall when/why I ended up getting this book (it appears to be one of the ones that has hung out in my to-be-read shelves for over a decade!), but I decided I'd check it out at this point.

This book started out with a lot of "resonances" for me that made me wonder if the authors had been with the Process Church ... they describe the mundane world as "grey" at a couple of points, they reference the work of Adler, they describe systems very close to "God patterns", and, heck, one of their *names* is the same as DeGrimston was born with! This never "went anywhere" that looked familiar, but it was *striking*, if only as coincidence.

Speaking of "never going anywhere", my main gripe with the book is that they spend 94% of it "defining the problem" and only 6% (of a rather skimpy 156 pages) making suggestions about *what to do about it* (ending with one "exercise", and three "approaches"), which makes this read more like a guidebook for setting up men's workshops than anything else! Also, the book is "very 80's", with frequent references to the original *Star Wars* and some global issues that sound mighty dated at this point.

That said, their premise *is* fascinating, arguing that our current society is developmentally stunted, frozen into "boy psychology" rather than "man psychology". As one would expect, King, Warrior, Magician, Lover[3] deals with how those "masculine archetypes" are actualized in both adolescent and mature forms. They present a graphic representation of this, as two nested pyramids, each with four faces. Each of those faces has three points, the top being the "fully actualized" archetype, and the other two being the bi-polar "shadow" of the archetype, with dysfunctional manifestations, one weak and one strong. An example of this would be in The King's triangle, with the "actualized" King at the apex with "The Tyrant" and "The Weakling" at the other points. As an example of how the "boy psychology" evolves to "man psychology", the "Hero" archetype matures into "The Warrior", with similar shifts in the "shadow".

Now, on the surface, a lot of this sounds like so much newage blithering, however, as the "shadow" attributes are detailed, I doubt any man reading this would not feel uncomfortable flashes of recognition of how those dysfunctional patterns manifest in his psychology. What the authors argue, of course, is that we ALL are stunted in our growth from boy to man ... largely because our civilization has lost the initiating functions of earlier tribal societies ... there are no more "Wise Men" or "Elders" who *know* to guide us into fully realized Manhood. This is why the lack of "what then?" material is so frustrating here ... it's a bit like a doctor looking at an x-ray, telling you that you have a worrisome lump, and then sending you home with an aspirin! The authors have, of course, spun out a number of additional books (one series with a book on working with each of the archetypes), lecture videos, workshops, etc., but it seems a bit like "cheating" to not have a good section of "what then" material in this one.

Despite my irritation with the "leaving the reader hanging" aspects, I do recommend this for the very interesting analysis of the male psyche. I'm sure I'm going to have issues raised in this kicking around in my head for *months*. It appears that this is still in print ... Amazon has it (at a 34% discount) at a bit over ten bucks and you can snag a "like new" copy from the new/used vendors for about three (plus shipping) ... but you could probably find this at your local bookstore as well if it sounds like somewhere you want to go.

Notes:

1. http://btripp-books.livejournal.com/17350.html
2-3. http://amzn.to/2cnU93y

Tuesday, May 9, 2006[1]

Fascinating ...

OK, so I probably have three or four other version of the Tao Te Ching in my library ... I *was* a Religion Major, after all ... but this one took me by surprise. As usual, I'm not sure when/why this got added into my to-be-read shelves, but it dates back to my P.R. days when I was making a lot of money and spending a good chunk of that on books and art (*damn*, I miss having money!). I also really can't say what made me "slot this in" at this point, except that I've gotten to a point in my to-be-read shelves where I have four or five "themes" (with a hefty stack of books each), none of which I've much felt like diving into at present, so I've been sort of "cherry picking" from the rest.

What makes Victor H. Mair's Tao Te Ching: The Classic Book of Integrity and the Way by Lao Tzu[2] particularly fascinating is his suggestion that the material collected in the Tao Te Ching (from previous oral traditions) has its roots in Indian yogic texts, specifically the Bagavad-Gita and the Upanishads. Obviously, this is the sort of claim that one would expect from "Llewellyn authors" and other newagers, but Mair is an A-list expert, Professor of Chinese Language and Literature in the Department of Oriental Studies at the University of Pennsylvania, and is considered one of America's foremost translators of ancient Chinese. So, when he writes something (from the Afterword) like:

> *"There are so many correspondences between Yoga and Taoism -- even in the smallest and oddest details -- throughout the history of their development that we might almost think of them as two variants of a single religious and philosophical system."*

... one needs to pay a certain degree of attention! His extensive translation notes frequently point out parallel passages from the Indian canon, and in the Appendix devoted to the subject, he traces out a possible timeline for how the ideas embodied in Indian Yoga could have found their way eventually into the Taoist writings (interestingly, he additionally references other scholars' work linking Taoism to Sufism, thereby weaving the major "mystical traditions" into a web worthy of, and perhaps on some levels *validating*, the Theosophists of the previous century).

This version of the Tao Te Ching[3] is also notable on being based on the "Ma-wang-tui Manuscripts", silk scrolls uncovered in a 1973 Chinese archaeological dig, which pre-date the standard versions of the Tao Te Ching by half a millennia and so provide a *much* earlier (read: less messed-with) version of the sayings. The differences most obviously manifest in the order of the book, starting with the "Te" (chapter 38 and following in the "traditional" version) and then going into the "Tao", or as Mair suggests, being more a "Te Tao Ching" (which he would translate as the "Integrity Way" book).

Needless to say, I would recommend this book to anybody who has an interest in Taoism, Chinese Literature, or how spiritual traditions interact with each other. Not surprisingly, this is still in print, and Amazon has it at a 35% discount for under ten bucks (and you could snag a "like new" copy for just over a buck through their new/used vendors) ... but it's yet another that could likely be had at from your local bookstore.

Notes:

1. http://btripp-books.livejournal.com/17517.html

2-3. http://amzn.to/2cnTuz6

Sunday, May 14, 2006[1]

Some poetry (not mine) ...

I have been a fan of Leonard Cohen for a very long time. Vinyl records ... remember them? I have most of the old stuff ... a half a dozen or so records from the late 60's and the 70's ... plus a number of the later albums on CD (I was interested to note that most if not all of his old albums have been released on CD). I've read books about him before, but I'm pretty sure this is the first actual collection of his poetry that I've read.

Now, one *would think* that, given the above, I'd be *raving* about Leonard Cohen's Stranger Music: Selected Poems and Songs[2], being that it is a voluminous look at his career. It not only has most of the lyrics to most of the albums (maybe all, I didn't check), but also reproduces the poetry collections from which he initially derived acclaim (*The Spice-Box of Earth*, etc.). Unfortunately, I find myself in the uncomfortable position of, perhaps, being *less of a fan* than I had been previously. Yes, he has his moments of brilliance. Yes, he is able to weave religion and war and conflict and sex into a fascinating fabric, but ... it somehow worked better for me a few pieces at a time on an album side.

Frankly, I'm guessing half of his poems are about getting laid, obsessing about women who he wants to screw, has screwed, or who are screwing other people behind his back, etc. etc. etc. It starts out *romantic*, perhaps *bohemian* (after all, that was the vibe from the early album covers' art/copy), but it soon enough becomes *irritating* and threatens to be perceived as *puerile* over the course of hundreds of poems. Sure, he may of had more sex in a year than I've had in my *life*, but I don't need to have my nose rubbed in it ... Reading Stranger Music[3] was a bit like talking to an old college buddy of mine (who would typically bed 3-5 different gals a week), at some point you really wish you could *change the subject* to something other than who/how/where/when he'd "gotten it wet"!

Still, most of the poems are pretty amazing. I do wish, however, that there had been some sort of over-all editorial framework ... intro bits that would say that so-and-so section was based on the such-and-such album from X year, or that it was a collection that was released in Y year and won various awards, etc. Being familiar with Cohen's music and history, I was able to more-or-less triangulate this info, but there were bits that would have been better with some explanation. This primarily applies to the "Death of a Lady's Man" section (not to be confused with the "Death of a Ladies' Man" section which was poems from the album of that name) which had intermittent "commentary" attached to various poems, but it appears (from the one brief note that *is* in the book) that some of those commentaries have been re-framed as poems for this edition, etc. ... plus the fact that these "commentary" bits are in a particularly sarcastic 3rd person talking about Cohen, which is rather confusing.

Anyway ... if you like Leonard Cohen, you *might* like this volume. If you've just *heard of* Leonard Cohen (and maybe know a few of his songs), I think you have a better chance of liking Stranger Music[4]. It appears that this is out of print, but you can get it via the Amazon new/used vendors in "very good" condition for about $7.00 (it was originally $24 when it came out in 1993). If you really want a "new" copy, though, you'll have to cough up a hundred bucks ... go figure!

Notes:

1. http://btripp-books.livejournal.com/17716.html

2-4. http://amzn.to/2cp19zV

Monday, May 15, 2006[1]

The first of three ...

I've had three of the "Collectors Library of the Unknown" books sitting around on my to-be-read shelves for a long time. This was a series that Time/Life did back in the early 90's where they re-printed "classics" of the genre in fancy hardbound silver-edged, purple "bookmark" ribboned, editions for who knows how much per copy (back in my P.R. days I spent a lot of money on books, and even had a rep from Time/Life who'd call me up monthly to see what they could sell me!). I eventually got "claustrophobic" with that arrangement and cut off all the series that I'd been getting, so this stopped at 3 books. For some reason, they seemed to be the sort of "break" that I needed between other stuff right now, so that's what's currently being read.

The first of these is J. Allen Hynek's seminal The UFO Experience: A Scientific Inquiry[2], the book which coined the "Close Encounter" classification scheme. Originally published in 1972, this book covered Hynek's years as a "scientific advisor" to the Air Force's "Project Blue Book", which was the official "clearinghouse" for info on UFO's. Hynek was not a "UFO buff" when he got involved in this, he was the chief astronomer running Ohio State's observatory at the time that the Air Technical Intelligence Center was being run out of Wright-Patterson AFB in Dayton ... they needed an astronomer to say "the observer was seeing Venus", and he was the nearest "A-list" specialist, and for 22 years (1947-1969, through "Project Sign", "Project Grudge" and "Project Blue Book") he was their "scientific advisor".

Hynek, was, however, *a scientist* (he ended up in a tenured "chair" position at Northwestern, after all), and he was *aghast* at what he saw happening in the Air Force's approach to the whole UFO issue. The UFO Experience[3] (which is, by the way, still in print in a paperback edition) was his "uncovering" of how badly managed the "official government response" to UFO phenomena had been, as well as his suggestions as to how to classify/approach future incidents.

Being from 1972, the book has certain "quaint" aspects ... it is easy to forget today how recently computer access has spread to the general population. One of his repeated pleas was to get the reports into "machine readable" format, which in those days (which I recall from my own highschool years) involved punching cards, which then were processed to punch a paper tape, which then was fed into a machine which sent *that* data over a phone line to "a computer" which would likely store the information on magnetic tape reels. This does beg the question, however, of why there haven't been HUGE strides in UFO research over, say, the past 20 years when computers have become more and more ubiquitous ... using Hynek's "Strangeness" and "Probability" ratings and his "prototype" classifications (nocturnal lights, daylight disks, radar-visual, and Close Encounters of the 1st, 2nd, and 3rd kinds), one would think that scientifically-minded "UFO buffs" would have by now amassed quite a dramatic amount of data. As Hynek points out, even the *Blue Book* (which existed largely to explain away all reports) had something like 25% "unidentified" sightings, but I can't say that I've seen much *convincing* material along these lines of recent vintage.

Also, Hynek was writing in a pre-"X-Files" world. From his perspective, most of what was wrong with the "official government approach" was due to institutional factors which arose more out of ignorance of "scientific approaches" and bias against the topic of UFOs in general, than any *conspiracy* to "cover up the truth". He details how frequently incidents with a LOT of data, many eye-witnesses, etc. were simply ignored, or only barely investigated ... the interest in the Air Force being to find the quickest route to "explain away" the event. However, there was ONE case which made me think of today's "paranoia" mode, in which he notes that a "government investigator" (in plain clothes, but who was recognized as an Air Force officer) had gone on-scene to interview witnesses *before* the incident had been officially reported ... from Hynek's perspective in 1972 it's "odd", from today's standpoint it *does* make one wonder if there was a whole separate secret group in the Air Force which was actually *studying* these events, and allowing Blue Book to run it's bumbling whitewash program as "cover".

Anyway, it was an interesting read, and if you have an interest in UFOs, you should have this book. As I noted, this is a fancy-schmancy edition, and it is, amazingly, available for as little as $2.75 for a "new" copy via Amazon's new/used vendors (although you could get a "good/acceptable" copy of the paperback for as little as 1¢, compared to the current paperback edition's cover price of $12.95), which seems like a pretty good deal!

Notes:

1. http://btripp-books.livejournal.com/17989.html
2-3. http://amzn.to/2bNMpsE

Friday, June 9, 2006[1]

Here's number two ...

I really do try to get these reviews written as soon as possible after reading a book, so most of the details (and brilliant observations I've made) are fresh in my mind. Unfortunately, I finished up this one on the morning of the day we lost power here, and we didn't get it back for 8 days, so this is a little "staler" than I'd prefer. Oh, well.

Speaking of "stale" (oh, that's a cheap shot), Harry Price's The Most Haunted House in England: Ten Years' Investigation of Borley Rectory[2] originally came out in 1940, with most of the material in the book amassed over the decade of the 1930's. Needless to say, it's almost as interesting as a "peek into the past" as it is for the ghost hunting! The edition in hand, of course, is from the 1989 "Collector's Library of the Unknown" series that Time/Life Books put out (with silver edges and purple bookmark ribbons). I subscribed to that series for a bit, figured that they were charging *way* too much, and canceled after 3 titles ... however, for purposes of "library continuity", I decided to read them all at a go, so they'd stay together on the shelf, with this being the second volume.

It helps to appreciate the milieu in which Harry Price operated if one has read a lot of Theosophical stuff. In pre-WW2 Europe there were many threads of "genteel mysticism" with Societies set up to study various phenomenon. The "ghost hunting" in this book is much more in this vein than the current "let's use infrared cameras and freak out at the slightest thing" TV genre. Price and his various collaborators took detailed notes, dutifully chalk-circling items on shelves, putting threads across doorways, and noting the appearances of even the tiniest markings on walls. It was all very *scientific*, of course.

The book focuses on the Borley Rectory, a rather large, rambling house supposedly built on the ruins of an old monastery. It seems to have been haunted by at least one ghost, purported to be the spirit of a nun, and possibly by some additional spirits of later owners of the house. Despite all the "research", the best information that Price & co. got seems to have been from a series of séances in which they communicate with these spirits (although the "most dramatic" material is the scrawled messages on the walls, and the many "poltergeist" phenomenon reported). Now, these days "séance" materials would be likely rejected out of hand as "evidence", but the approach was much in vogue at the time.

What I found *quite* frustrating in Price's accounts was that they never *took action* to even attempt to meet the spirits' requests. Again, the "Nun" was the longest-reported haunting, and their research indicated that she'd been killed and buried in a shallow grave in a particular place outside the house. Both the wall scrawlings and the séance materials ("knock once for yes, twice for no" sorts of things plus a tiresome run-through-the-alphabet thing to have stuff spelled out) indicated that this spirit was simply looking for a proper Catholic *burial* service, but it didn't seem to occur to anybody to go about arranging for this to be attempted! At the end of his 10-year investigation, Price seemed to pretty much wash his hands of the project, only returning after a fire gutted the house some years later (and even *then* there was no attempt to put at least that one spirit to rest).

Oddly enough, it seems that most of the poltergeist phenomenon were due to the ghost of one of the house's previous owners, who had himself dedicated quite a lot of time to researching the ghosts! While I'm no *expert* in this particular genre, it would seem to me that the later ghost was trying very hard to draw attention to the plight of the *earlier* spirit, and BOTH of them could move on if they'd just rung up the local Cardinal's office and requested their best "minister to the disincarnate" to come out and have a go with some Latin, incense, and holy water!

Anyway ... I guess this is a "classic" of the ghost-hunting genre, and if it's your thing, you'd probably like it quite a lot ... if it's not your thing, your mileage may vary ... I found it interesting enough as a "time capsule" from a more genteel era that it seemed worth the reading. The Most Haunted House in England[3] is, not surprisingly, out of print, but copies of this edition *are* available via Amazon's new/used vendors for as little as $2.99 ... which is about 1/10th of what I paid for it (if I'm recalling correctly) new ... and "new" copies are out there for not much more, if you want it in tidy shape.

Notes:

1. http://btripp-books.livejournal.com/18252.html

2-3. http://amzn.to/2cyslgE

Friday, June 9, 2006[1]

While I'm at it ...

Like the previous review, I've been done with this book for over a week at this point, so some of the "immediacy" of my reactions to the book have faded. However, this, too, has its "quaint" moments. Frankly, reading Louisa E. Rhine's Hidden Channels of the Mind[2], I couldn't shake the images of the first *GhostBusters* movie, as in this book she *assumes* that by now *every* major university would have a Parapsychology program like that which her husband had set up at Duke. If the name is familiar, it's because J.B. Rhine developed the "Zener" cards as perhaps *the* classic lab experiment for ESP. While Parapsychology *is* recognized as a *science* by the American Association for the Advancement of Science, it's hardly *generally* recognized as such, and the stance taken by Louisa Rhine in this 1961 book (in which Parapsychology is discussed as an "emerging science" akin to, say, Robotics) seems "long ago and far away". Frankly, I wonder "what went wrong?", but fear the answer is that Psi did not translate sufficiently well to the laboratory to make it supportable in the halls of academia.

Unfortunately, Hidden Channels of the Mind[3] is neither a *provocative* look at ESP/Psi, nor is it a particularly *rigorous* look at the phenomenon, but seems to float in a middle ground, with a formal structure, but heavily based on unattributed "stories", many of which reminded me of those Angel books I read a month or so back! I hate to just walk you thought the contents page, but "cherry picking" some highlights might well be the best way to show where the author was going in this book. She discusses "Types of Extrasensory Perception", divided into "from other minds", "from mindless objects" and "from the future", then looks at the "Forms of ESP Experience" which she splits into "realistic", "unrealistic", "hallucinatory" and "intuitive". A section looks at space and time, another looks at the difference of how men and women perform in lab tests, and another looks at performance across various age ranges ... again, these would be a lot more interesting (to me at least) if they focused on the lab results, but they're primarily *stories* of so-and-so "seeing" such-and-such, but none in a lab setting. The second half of the book is largely set on precognition, with a whole section looking at whether one can or can not avoid "foreseen" events ... unfortunately, here too, the bulk of the "evidence" is tales of distraught mothers/wives wondering if they could have "done something" (or tales of them having prevented loved ones from "getting on that train", etc.) ... needless to say, this sounds pretty weak nearly fifty years down the road.

This is not to say that the book is not worth a read, it's just not the book I'd hope it would be ... if the Rhines had taken the "scientific rigor" that Hynek applied to his UFO studies, ESP might have had a more solid foundation to grow on, but if all their work depended on the sort of "evidence" that's presented here, it's understandable why Parapsychology sort of faded away as a "respectable" field of study!

While this one is officially out of print, the Amazon new/used vendors have "like new" copies available for under a buck ... and given that these are such swank editions (silver edging, purple ribbon book marker, etc.), you might want to snag one just for the heck of it.

Notes:

1. http://btripp-books.livejournal.com/18661.html
2-3. http://amzn.to/1QSoSE5

Monday, June 12, 2006[1]

Nothing like old predictions ...

OK, so this is "one of those books" ... something that I felt I *ought* to read, but really *should* have read a decade ago. In my defense, however, I'll note that this is one of the books that I wanted to read which I "cherry picked" from my Mom's library when we were finally clearing out her place (she'd been an early Microsoft stockholder), so it's not been languishing on *my* shelves for much more than a year.

Needless to say, even the most accurate prognosticator is likely to be somewhat uncomfortable with his predictions a decade down the line, but I'm sure that Bill Gates is pretty proud of how often he was *right* in The Road Ahead[2], his book about The Internet. One has to recall that the Web was in its *infancy* when this book came out in 1995. Heck, HTML wasn't around until 1992, and only started appearing in the U.S. in 1993, so this book was *very* forward-looking for its time (I'd like to note that I created the old Eschaton Books web site in April of 1996, so I wasn't *too* far behind the curve, just way less well-funded!).

One thing that reading this book has done for me is to put some of the news stories of the past decade into perspective ... remember the big stink about Gates wanting to put a whole network of satellites in orbit? In the book he talks about a plan to put up 1,000 low-orbit satellites to provide wireless connectivity anywhere on the planet (a plan that got scuttled in the post-Columbia slow-down, but could well be revived given the new "commercial" space options). The press reported it like it was some form of megalomania, but he makes a very good case for it in the book. There are a number of similar examples of "oh, so *that's* what was going on!" revelations, but this is the one that comes first to mind.

If anything, Gates paints "too rosy" a picture of the "the future" ... one thing he totally missed was the "pirate culture" and how pervasive it would be. He talks about *piracy*, but only in the context of software licensing, he obviously didn't foresee how colleges would make high-speed connections available to their students, and how these students would set up file-sharing systems to illegally distribute copyrighted material, and how the Music (and, later, Movie) Industry would respond to the culture of Intellectual Property Theft that would emerge from that file-sharing. Gates' version saw the Music Industry working out a sane "personal license" system where people would buy, for a quarter or so, "personal use rights" to particular tracks ... of course, the "horse was out of the barn" before the Music Industry took the Web seriously, and so the story of "entertainment" on the Web has been more of a prolonged court battle than anything else.

Another place where Gates' vision diverges from what's happened (so far) is in the level of "interconnectivity" ... as anybody who has used Windows since 3.1 knows, at every step Microsoft has tried to make the "computer experience" one big unified *thing*, attempting to blur the lines between text, spreadsheet, database, graphics, video, Web, etc. ... this is very much part of his "vision", where individual computers are just "access points" to a bigger, more intertwined, "Information Highway" ... and is something to which I believe there is a *lot* of resistance. He does, however, describe in eerie accuracy the new generation of "phones" that have full use of computer functions like MS Office (and GPS tracking) in what he describes as "Wallet PCs" ... however, these have not quite become the "Big Brother" tool (keeping all one's personal data, one's "music licenses", one's credit card or PayPal-esque info, etc.) that he seems to be heading for.

Would I recommend The Road Ahead[3], especially at this point? Maybe ... I mean, I've been involved with developing Web sites for a decade, so I've sort of watched as this stuff has played out, and it's interesting to compare my recall to what Gates was forecasting ... however, for the "uninvolved reader" it might sound a bit like the typical *"oooh, we'll have flying cars by 1979!"* sort of "futurism", with many "reality paths" verging off (for whatever reason) from what Gates was guessing back in 1995. The good news is that if you *are* interested in reading this, it's available for cheap from the Amazon new/used vendors, with "like new" copies going for as little as 1¢ (plus $3.49 shipping, of course), and copies that still have the CD for as low as 25¢, and "new" copies starting at a buck ... such a deal!

Notes:

1. http://btripp-books.livejournal.com/18934.html

2-3. http://amzn.to/2bNLsRr

Thursday, June 15, 2006[1]

(heavy sigh) ... this one hit home ...

This book, like its predecessor in my review stream, came from my late Mother's library, or what remained of it at her death (she had previously donated her vast cooking/culinary collection to a college). I'd "cherry-picked" this as something to come home with me (rather than to storage) because I rather like these "A Life In Food" memoirs, and there were pictures in it of all sorts of people I knew growing up.

However, I did not anticipate just what a *difficult* read James Villas' Between Bites: Memoirs of a Hungry Hedonist[2] would be for me. Not, certainly, for the density of the prose, but nearly every page brought up reminders of who I used to be, and how much I have lost. Villas was the food and wine editor of Town & Country magazine for 27 years and wrote for many other magazines as well ... his book traces his life through the explosion of the "cuisine craze" of the 1960's and his professional involvement in it from the 70's on.

My Mother had been in Advertising and PR (primarily for major food clients) in New York in the 50's and 60's, moving out to Chicago in the late 60's ... all my Mom's best buddies, the "food elite" of the era, Michael Field, James Beard, Julia Child, Craig Claiborne, Joe Baum, Barbara Kafka, etc., etc., etc., figure in the story, and very much in *my* history (we were at a fundraiser in NYC one time in the 80's when either Tom Margittai or Paul Kovi asked, incredulously, about me *"Is **this** what I used to lift into the kiddie seats up at Tower Suite???"*), including the many other names that I worked with, Paul Prudhomme, Wolfgang Puck, Leslee Reis, Jane & Michael Stern, Martha Stewart, etc., when a Vice President in my Mom's firm through the 80's and 90's, not to *mention* the dozens of other restaurateurs we patronized, not the least of which, Jovan Trboyevic, whose incomparable *Le Perroquet* was just downstairs from our offices, allowing my Mother to spoil our clients (and herself, typically lunching there 2-3 times a week) with some of the best food on the planet, with no more logistical headaches than running them through "the company cafeteria".

When I read Villas' stories, it brings back my childhood in New York, it brings back a flood of amazing food memories, and it reminds me of what was great about my old job in Public Relations. And, given how things have gone in my life, all that *hurts like hell*.

Anyway ... it is (obviously) difficult for me to disengage "my memories" from "his memoirs" ... suffice it to say, this is a well-written book, with much humor, a couple of dozen amazing recipes, and stories about a world that is now, sadly, somewhat behind us all (this is not to say that *today* is not a "popular renaissance" for *cuisine*, but it's in a sound-bite Food Channel form that lacks the grace and certainty of the shining lights of the post-WW2 decades). Villas, while still quite active writing, is now strictly free-lance, and seems to be glad to be relieved of the chore of reviewing "the latest hot sushi bar". If you have any interest in fine dining, and/or the development of the modern Culinary genre, I would heartily recommend picking up a copy of <u>Between Bites</u>[3], as it is certainly provides a window in on that world.

As this is a relatively recent book (the paperback I have came out in 2002), it's still in print, so should be available at your local Big Book Store were you kindly interested in providing Mr. Villas with some royalties. Copies of the *hardcover* edition, however, can be had for a pittance through the Amazon new/used vendors, with "like new" copies going for as little as $1.57 (plus shipping, of course). Again, I do recommend this for those interested, and I hope that all out there will forgive the massively run-on nature of the third paragraph (where I tackle six different issues in one badly-in-need-of-editing sentence).

Notes:

1. http://btripp-books.livejournal.com/19172.html

2-3. http://amzn.to/2cnPRck

Wednesday, June 28, 2006[1]

Oh, look ... a book!

Gee, it seems to *me* like I haven't knocked down a book in *ages*, but since nobody bothers to read these things, I guess it's a moot issue. Actually, the "read date[2]" for this is two weeks past the previous, so that it rather a long time for me to go between books, but given the Major Project last week, I got next to no reading done.

Once again, I'm plowing into a series of books here ... again from my book buying days in the early 90's, and again from Time-Life. These are four books from their "Lost Civilizations" series, which is really quite well done. This volume, The Celts: Europe's People of Iron[3] takes a look at the iron-age Celtic cultures across Europe in the first millennium B.C.E.

The "Lost Civilization" series is interesting in that, while hardly being *academic*, is very well researched, and extensively illustrated ... rarely is a key artifact mentioned without being pictured, which helps one "experience" the information. While brief (each is about 160 pages), each volume tackles its subject in some breadth, and the books are somewhat reminiscent of a museum guide book produced for a themed exhibit.

While I've read a goodly amount of Celtic historical stuff (ala Pagan Celtic Ireland[4] a number of weeks back) which has gone into more *detail*, The Celts: Europe's People of Iron[5] provides a wider perspective, discussing cultural remains from Spain to Turkey to Ireland. Because the Celts didn't leave written records (the Druids forbade the non-verbal transmission of their knowledge, and it was only after Rome's conquests that some of this material was set to paper), didn't (generally) build major enduring stone edifices, and typically practiced cremation (leaving few "rich tombs"), their culture, spanning all of Northern Europe for a thousand years, is largely only known from outside sources and few "fortunate" survivals of ritual sites.

This book looks at these various materials, and discusses the major figures who researched the Celts over the past several centuries. Again, this is hardly a college course on the Celtic World, but I felt it was a very decent over-view of the subject, which put the culture of the Celts into historical context and provided insights into their economy, art, and religion that would be hard to get without a lot of museum visiting! While being out of print, copies in various conditions can be had from the Amazon new/used vendors for as little as $1.30 ... if you're interested in learning about the Celtic culture, this would be a good one to pick up!

Notes:
1. http://btripp-books.livejournal.com/19264.html
2. http://btripp-books.com
3. http://amzn.to/2bUbpNP
4. http://btripp-books.livejournal.com/16679.html
5. http://amzn.to/2bUbpNP

Thursday, June 29, 2006[1]

and, another book ...

Well, *that* was more like it ... it really bugged me that I got "stuck" the past couple of weeks with very little reading getting done, and I was able to knock down this book in just a couple of days! Part of this might be due to my being fairly familiar with much of the subject matter ... I had a lot of "been there!" moments going through the various archaeological sites in this book from my many trips to Mexico back in the 80's and 90's.

Another title from the Time-Life ""Lost Civilizations" series, Aztecs: Reign of Blood and Splendor[2] is an interesting over-view of the Aztecs, and their regional predecessors. One thing that this book did was put a focus on the chronological context for much of the cultures in central Mexico ... despite how many times I've been there, I've always "filed" these sites in time slots much earlier than they actually arose. After all, it's not been quite 500 years since the Spanish took Tenochtitlan and destroyed the Aztec empire ... and the "mythic era" of Teotihuacan was somewhere around 100 CE, which was the same era as Trajan was emperor of Rome, 12 rulers past Caesar ... which in the *western* cultural time-line is, if not "yesterday", at least in a very easily conceptualized period. Somehow the vast metropolis of the Aztec capitol always seemed a more distant thing.

Like the Celtic book that I reviewed a day or so ago, this is heavily illustrated, bringing together materials from dozens of museums, etc., which certainly helps "bring home" the elements of the culture. Of course, most of the materials have had to come from archaeological kismet, as nearly all of the documentation from the Aztecs was destroyed in a campaign of cultural obliteration by the Catholic Church, and very nearly all gold, silver, and gemwork was purloined by the Spanish. Fortunately, in recent decades many significant finds have been made from the old Aztec capitol that escaped the monks and soldiers.

Frankly, there is a lot of unsettling material in here ... the Aztecs were "not nice people" by our own cultural standards, working in a mythos that demanded almost constant human sacrifice, which drove a culture that was militarized in such a way to provide a never-ending stream of captives to kill ... and the writers don't spare their readers much in terms of graphic descriptions. Again, I'd "been aware" of much of the material here, but it was quite an eye-opener to see it all presented as it was, and most of it was placed within a more in-depth cultural context than I'd seen it before.

Like the rest of the series, Aztecs: Reign of Blood and Splendor[3] is out-of-print now, but you can get a "like new" copy from the Amazon new/used vendors for as little as a penny ... so if you'd like to take an unblinking look at the Aztec culture, you could pick this up for next to nothing! If I didn't have it already, I'd jump on that.

Notes:

1. http://btripp-books.livejournal.com/19557.html   2-3. http://amzn.to/2cnNpSV

Sunday, July 9, 2006[1]

or, "Dude, Where's My Car?" by any other name ...

OK, so that's assuming one drives an *El Dorado* (yuk, yuk, yuk). But seriously, folks ... The Search For El Dorado[2] is a very interesting book. Frankly, I was sort of expecting a "cultural milieu of the Incas" book, but this actually only peripherally touches on the Incas, and looks instead at various cultures which preceded them in South America, plus the Spanish (and others') search for the mythical "City of Gold".

Oddly enough, it appears that there was a "core truth" behind the myth of El Dorado ... only it got blown up way out of perspective in various re-tellings ... there was a South American culture where the King, on certain ceremonial occasions, was coated head-to-toe with gold dust adhered to him with some sort of resin, he would be taken out on a raft into the middle of this lake, and would dive in, washing off the gold, and priests and other officiants would also throw in gold objects and emeralds. Well, this eventually became told as a *daily* routine, and rather than being part of an otherwise rather ordinary pre-Iron-Age setting, the re-telling built the whole city into gold streets, palaces, etc. The location, amazingly, has even been pretty well determined, and the lake has been drained, dredged, dived in, etc. repeatedly, frequently turning up just enough gold to keep folks coming. Of course, the *Spanish* fully bought into the "big gold city" thing, and were charging around all over the place, butchering locals who wouldn't tell them where "The Gold City" was, and generally creating massive carnage in the name of their God and Crown.

The first part of the book looks at these various searches, and then it settles in at considering the locals on a rather long scale of 10,000 bce to the 1600's and the post-Conquest chaos. Major sections are given over to discussing the Chavin, the Moche, and the Paracas/Nazca cultures, although attention is also given to the Muisca, the Chimu, the Tiahuanaco, the Wari, and various other groups which preceded the Incas. As much of the traces of these cultures were obliterated by the Spanish, most of what is known of them is pieced together from what burials have *not* been destroyed by the "professional grave robbers" so prevalent in Latin countries. Fortunately, enough seems to have survived to paint a reasonable picture of each of these groups.

Again, I was surprised by the focus of The Search For El Dorado[3] (I only have 4 of the "Lost Civilizations" series, out of at least 16, and one of the others *was* about the Incas), and found it very informative in an area that that I had some passing familiarity, but very little in-depth information. These are out of print at this point, so if you'd like a copy, you're looking at the Amazon new/used vendors (or their equivalent elsewhere) ... you can get one for as little as 36¢ (plus shipping) for a copy in "good" condition, and can have a "like new" copy starting around a buck fifty. If this sounds like something you'd like to read up on, I'd certainly tell you to go grab a copy over there!

Notes: 1. http://btripp-books.livejournal.com/19740.html   2-3. http://amzn.to/2cnNtSO

Thursday, July 13, 2006[1]

The last of these ...

OK, so here's the fourth of those "Lost Civilization" series books that I'd gotten from Time-Life back in the early 90's. Egypt: Land of the Pharaohs[2] shares many aspects with the previous three titles I've read/reviewed from the series (as one might expect, having the same editor, Dale M. Brown, supervising their production), in that they do an interesting job of putting a lot of details into a wider perspective, and highlighting this with extensive art/photography. This is certainly not an "in-depth" look at ancient Egypt (see my *next* review for one of those), but it does a decent job of presenting the Western discovery of it, an overview of the history, and several interesting "technical" side bits on various subjects.

The one gripe that I had was that the last third of the book was pretty much all Tutankhamun ... sure, his relatively unsullied burial chambers (interestingly, a factoid that I'd not been aware of, it *had* been robbed in antiquity, but only of jewelry, etc.) provide a fascinating window into the ancient world, but he was a minor figure (frankly, his name barely shows up in the King lists) in a transitional time. One point they make which I found of note was that due to the wealth and power of Egypt at the time Tutankhamun reigned, the grave goods he had could well be of the highest quality, and that other more famous Pharaoh's tombs might not have had much more impressive things than were found in this one.

I have to admit, that I've been reading *another* book on ancient Egypt while plowing through these four "Lost Civilization" books, so my *impressions* from this one on Egypt are less clear than the ones on other cultures, so most of what I'm coming up with to write about it are a bit muddled with the other book, as well as with the dozens of books I've read on the subject previously!

Anyway, Egypt: Land of the Pharaohs[3] was not a *bad* read ... aside from the caveat noted above, it was an enjoyable and informative (within its scope) book. If you have an interest in a heavily-illustrated volume that still provides useful data on ancient Egypt, you might well take a look at picking up a copy of this. Again, these are out of print, so you'd be looking to the new/used secondary market, but the Amazon guys have it "new" for under a buck (not bad given its initial $29.95 cover price!), so even with shipping it's a steal.

Notes:

1. http://btripp-books.livejournal.com/20135.html
2-3. http://amzn.to/2bKu4OZ

Friday, July 14, 2006[1]

Yeah, another one ...

As I noted in my last review, I was reading *another* book on Egypt while plowing through those four "Lost Civilizations" books. This one was also part of a series, "The Cultural Atlas of the World", and I figured it would take as long, in parallel, to read it as those four books, and they did, indeed, come in at a dead heat.

John Baines & Jaromir Malek's Ancient Egypt[2] is a remarkable book. I'd not seen any of the "Cultural Atlas" books, but I assume they're all based on this concept, of taking the *geography* of the studied region to act as a framework for the cultural aspects. Of course, for *Egypt* this is a remarkably revealing approach, starting in far Upper (South-ern) Egypt, the book walks the reader ruin site to ruin site all the way up to the Delta, describing the ancient Egyptians' political structures, dynastic struggles, and evolving civilization. The only downside of this is that most of the narrative didn't have a clear "time arrow", as it would move from one site from the Old Kingdom to one that primarily hailed from the Ptolemaic era, and much of this was discussed in terms of *Dynasties* rather than years, so one did have a tendency to lose track of what was from when. To be fair, the first quarter or so of the book *does* give a "historical portrait" of Egyptian civilization, so I suppose if one was to be referring back and forth (OK, or *paying more attention*) it would be less hazy than I experienced it.

There were several things that I found surprising, although in retrospect, I suppose they make sense ... prime among these is just how much Greco/Roman material there is .. of course, being the "later phase" this stuff has had less time to disappear, but given the thousands of years of building, it's just such a small slice. I was also surprised to find how many of the Roman Emperors added their touches to various sites. There was Hadrian's *this* and Trajan's *that*, and most of this stuff seemed to be additions or restorations to *Egyptian* temples honoring the local Gods, in the classic Egyptian style for the most part. Somehow I guess I though that if a Roman Emperor was going to build something it was going to look, well, *Roman* and be dedicated to their Gods. I suspect that this might come from too much Shakespeare as a source for my "Rome in Egypt" mental framework!

Ancient Egypt[3], being an *atlas* is chock-full of maps, perhaps giving the best sense of any source of exactly *where* the various *whats* are in Egypt, but aside from that it is "lavishly illustrated" with photos, line drawings, art reproductions, and diagrams. Personally, and this is just a gripe, I wish they'd invested in some fly-time to take aerial shots of more of the ruin sites, as after a while the dune-level snapshot of bits of columns or pylons got to be a bit of a blur, and having the bird's eye view would have made it a lot easier to "get" the many "site diagrams" they provided, which (for me at least) were often hard to mentally assemble the temple bits into.

These caveats aside, this is one heck of a *reference* to have handy, as it allows you to look up nearly *any* significant Egyptian ruin and get at least a thumbnail of what it was about. A later version[4] (from a different publisher) of Ancient Egypt[5] *is* still in print, but has a $50 cover price ... copies of the original version are available, though, via the Amazon new/used vendors in "like new" condition for as little as $3.99 ... which is what I'd be looking at if I were going to be picking up a copy.

Notes:

1. http://btripp-books.livejournal.com/20407.html
2-3. http://amzn.to/2bTAitb
4. http://amzn.to/2bTuy0C
5. http://amzn.to/2bTAitb

Saturday, July 15, 2006[1]

Wow ...

This is an *amazing* book ... due to my reading choices, I rarely hit a book that "I can't put down", but this came pretty close. Louis Palmer's Adventures in Afghanistan[2] (published in 1990) takes place in the post-Soviet/pre-Taliban years, where a puppet communist regime had a tenuous grasp on the country, and "the resistance" controlled much of its territory. This is, on the surface, a travelogue of the author accompanying Mujahidin fighters on a "supply run" through various parts of Afghanistan, under the "protection" of the Mu'assisa, the "Sufi central organization", but it is more a collection of vignettes where "ancient teaching stories" are presented to the reader. Frankly, despite my serious caveats below, I highly recommend this book to *anyone*.

The author describes fabulous scenes, hidden palaces cut into mountains, Alexander-era Greek cities sitting abandoned since being sacked by the Mongols, vast monasteries more complex and impressive than the Potala, standing forts in the style to the Taj Mahal ... he himself says he'd not believe the things he's seen had he not seen them. Incredible. And, unfortunately, that seems to be the sad fact here, it's *not* credible. As the book moves on a nagging voice starts up in the back of the head ... "how come I've never *heard* of any of these places?" ... "why are there no photos/sketches" ... "where exactly *are* these places?" ... none of these have answers. Also, a Google search for a "Louis Palmer" (coupled with "Sufi" or "Afghanistan") turns up *nothing* but references to the book ... who is this fellow, and what were his qualifications to get into a position to go on this hazardous yet wondrous journey?

As those who read these little reviews know, I've read quite a lot of Sufi material, primarily that coming from Idries Shah's Octagon Press, and it is always wise to take a step back from the "immediate impression" of this material and ask oneself, "What is being *achieved* by this book?". To be honest, I was buying everything here hook, line, and sinker for about the first 3/4 of the book, making notes of stuff that I wanted to research further (as frequent readers also know, I'm a "ruin junkie"), and wondering if it was safe to travel as a tourist in Afghanistan these days! I have also had quite a fascination about the "Sufi world", and have wondered how one could get hooked up with "the Mu'assisa" or something like it, the *true* source of these teachings, making me deeply hope that it was as easy as the author found it. I did, however, note how many of the various "teaching vignettes" really hit home with me, and came to realize, somewhere towards the end of the book, that this was no doubt the point. That this book was one of Shah's experiments in reaching out with *teachings* via a vehicle different from yet another Mullah Nasruddin book, or a look at Sufi activities in a particular culture.

That said, this is quite a tale, *especially* enticing to somebody with my interests. The author weaves a stunning tapestry of little factoids and histories that may or may not be *actual*, from the roots of Masonic ritual, the interrelationship of various Royal houses, the inter-play of Buddhist, Greek, and other cultures in the area, and an extraordinary string of descriptions of ruined cities, monasteries, palaces, fortresses, etc., etc., etc. in the virtually inaccessible reaches of Afghanistan. If even 10% of the travelogue is *true*, it provides tantalizing clues to much which the modern seeker might not even suspect, however the "payoff" is in the *teachings* which are discussions that the author reports having with numerous "wise" personages through his journey. The setting for each of these draws the reader in, and provides "conditions" for the story to have some impact. Of course, *"what do I know?"* ... for all I can *prove* every word that the elusive Mr. Palmer writes may well be factually true, but I strongly suspect the "fabulous" elements are the cheese in the trap, focusing the reader on what is being transmitted.

However, as I said above, I highly recommend Adventures in Afghanistan[3] to anybody, but especially to those who share my fascination with the general subject matter. Being that the book is from Octagon, it is still in print, but is (as nearly all their books are) *very* expensive. A new copy, either direct from them or from Amazon, etc., will set you back $35 for the 240-page hardcover (which I have) or $19 for the paperback. As is also frequently the case with Octagon titles, there aren't that many to be had in the new/used market, and the cheapest this could be had seems to be $7.20 for a used copy of the paperback. Either way, I believe that it would be money well spent.

Notes:

1. http://btripp-books.livejournal.com/20618.html
2-3. http://amzn.to/2bTASqT

Tuesday, July 18, 2006[1]

Hmmmmm ...

OK, so I obviously, somewhere back in the early 90's, bought a multiple-book bundle from Octagon about Afghanistan, which included the previous book reviewed here, as well as this and (what should be) the next two. I've been reading stuff from Octagon (primarily the works of Idries Shah), as well as from the Institute for Cultural Research, Designist Communications, and other of Shah's multiple projects for as long as 30 years now. And up till now I've never had any *substantial* reason to doubt any of what was coming out from those sources. However, in doing some background checking on this book, I ran into a few pieces on the Web which were quite anti-Shah, and I began to wonder. As I noted in my review of Adventures in Afghanistan, it was almost impossible to find any background on the putative author of that, or of much of what he describes. And, here too, My Life: From Brigand to King -- Autobiography of Amir Habibullah[2], while dealing with what do appear to be *historical figures* almost all of the names, when Googled, point only back to quotes from this book. This "autobiography" is of a man, Bacha Saquo (which *may* just mean "son of a water-carrier", which is what he initially was), who became a notorious bandit in post-British Afghanistan, eventually heading his own army and ousting the previous monarchy to install himself as King (in 1929) for a whole nine months. Notably, however, the "autobiography" was supposedly written by a Jamal Gul, a childhood friend of Bacha's who accompanied him through all the various adventures and perils of his life (while seemingly taking copious notes), yet somehow escapes execution (supposedly the fate of all of Bacha's henchmen), and manages to publish this "in Persian" some time afterwards (this being presented as a "translation"" of the original Persian book). However, again via Google, there seems to be no trace of the author nor the previous book prior to this ... not that is *ultimately* damning, there *is* a great abyss of non-web information on things prior to about 1995, after all, but it still seems odd. Some small voice in my head was wondering if this had been penned by Shah (or one of his associated group, something not unknown to the Octagon catalog), and was actually of only recent vintage.

None of this goes to say that My Life: From Brigand to King[3] is not a fascinating read, as it is quite the adventure tale, if a bit on the cruel and bloody side. It follows its protagonist from his extremely humble beginnings, into his initial entry in a life of murder and mayhem, through an ever-expanding series of criminal enterprises, and eventually to the Kingship (and his speedy downfall). Frankly, his character is painted in a way that immediately brought to mind some people that I've known from more-or-less that part of the world, so it had a glimmer of truth to it there. However, much seems difficult to believe here too, as his exploits are one "never before achieved" daring attack after another, always with intense bragging involved.

As I've noted before about Sufi books (and one has to assume that any book from Octagon has at least some Sufi subtext), one has to take a step back and try to see what's being *transmitted* along with the story ... and, frankly, I'm at a loss to identify what that would be in this book. There is *one* "magical" element, a talisman given to him (along with a prophesy of him becoming King) by a wandering Mullah, which is a constant part of his rise, but this is never particularly described, analyzed, nor discussed, just *mentioned* as a touch-stone of why he felt he could not be defeated. This hardly a teaching story makes. Aside from this, there was precious little else that I could point to and say "perhaps *this* is the real message", but perhaps I'm simply not seeing something that might be evident to somebody else.

Anyway, this is an OK book ... I really can't recommend you running out to buy it, though, unless you have a burning interest in (supposed) Afghan history, or are a big fan of this sort of literature. Being from Octagon, it is both still in print, and expensive ($30 in hardcover), and you're not saving much via the Amazon new/used vendors ($10.80 for a "like new" copy), so maybe look for it at your local used book store instead.

Notes:

1. http://btripp-books.livejournal.com/20829.html

2-3. http://amzn.to/2c2RnnB

Friday, July 21, 2006[1]

Another odd one ...

I guess it's possible, as in the famed Freud quote, "Sometimes a cigar is *just* a cigar.", that this (like the last reviewed book), is *just* an adventure story. There is precious little in Morag Murray Abdulah's My Khyber Marriage[2] to make one think that it is some sort of teaching parable. I do find it interesting, however, that this dates to the same time as the previous book[3] (the period after WW1), and wonder if there is some sort of information being "triangulated" by these publications.

As I've noted previously, it seems that Octagon (and Idries Shah's various other publishing ventures) rarely, if ever, put out material that does *not* in some way reflect Sufi teachings, or point to social elements which could indicate survivals or incursions of such teachings. These past few books on Afghanistan (or, in this case, the Pushtun tribal lands which the author distinguishes as separate from Afghanistan) seem to have no *overt* purpose in that direction. It did cross my mind that *perhaps* Shah was having these "antique" books reprinted in 1990 to provide some "background";. on the civil war then raging in his homeland. However, it would seem an odd approach to simply give airing to two views of traditional Afghan tribal existence (where a more expository book drawing on these and other sources might have been a more efficient route to that goal) if that was the case. Interestingly, Shah's own mother was a Scottish national who married into an Afghan family (in a similar time frame as the author's story), so it also occurred to me that this might be a "paraphrase" of his parents' early years together, presented in a fictionalized form, and not actually a book by the supposed author (although she does have *another* book, a follow-up to this, it was published in 1997 by Octagon, suggesting that it was probably *written* in the interim ... again, no trace of "the original publication" of either book seems to be out there).

Be that as it may, My Khyber Marriage[4] is interesting enough, providing a look at the "inner world" of the Afghan tribal culture, behind the fort walls, and in the "forbidden" women's quarters. As was the case in my previous review, I found many of the "exploits" in this just a bit too contrived ... it seems like the protagonist managed to "work wonders" in the social environment she was in, while defying her husband and father-in-law at nearly every turn to rush out on ill-advised adventures. Some of these were based around her wanting to see what was behind some of the "superstitions" of her Afghan family ... providing the only "mystical" elements in the book ... but all seemed slightly implausible given both the era and the setting. I don't know if this is to highlight them to point to a "message" or is simply a modern pen not taking full account of the mores of another time. The book also ends quite suddenly. The protagonist and her family go on an extended visit in India (with no seeming *point* except to perhaps put in some digs at both the British colonial system *and* the Hindus), an are at the last called back to Scotland where the book just stops, leaving the reader unfulfilled with the narrative.

As this is an Octagon book, it is still in print, and quite pricey ... $30 at retail, and not much better via the new/used vendors. As I suggested on the previous book, this is one that, were you for some reason interested in picking up, might be something to look for at your local used book store.

Notes:

1. http://btripp-books.livejournal.com/21121.html
2. http://amzn.to/2bLIM9p
3. http://btripp-books.livejournal.com/20829.html
4. http://amzn.to/2bLIM9p

Sunday, July 30, 2006[1]

Well, that's more like it!

This is the fourth of those four "Afghanistan" books that I'd gotten from Octagon back in the early 90's, and I'm glad that I held this one to last. As those who have been reading my recent reviews will recall, I've been having a hard time triangulating the other three books in terms of their veracity (having some serious doubts that the books are what they purport to be), and *purpose* (i.e., why Idries Shah wished to have them published at that particular time). This one, Afghan Caravan[2] (edited by Safia Shah), however, is quite the "typical" sort of Octagon book, where you can see the gears moving and many things working beneath the surface of the actual narratives! Interestingly, this is credited by Amazon as a book *by* Idries Shah, yet his daughter Safia's name is on the cover (as editor) and this does seem to be her project ... while a substantial part of the book is drawn from Idries Shah's writings (published and previously unpublished), it has many other authors included, Idries' father Sirdar Ikbal Ali Shah among them, as well as excerpts from a number of other Octagon books and bits and pieces of memoirs and travelogues published by visitors to and/or soldiers (from various countries) stationed in Afghanistan over the past hundred years or so.

Afghan Caravan[3] is set up in "thematic" sections, "Looking At Each Other" dealing with cross-cultural perceptions, "Wanderings" which are travel notes from various visitors (which includes a good deal of "fantastic" material), "Hows, Whys, Whats" that looks at a wide range of topics from making rice to carpet expertise to the use of formal titles, etc., "Heard In The Tea-House" which is a group of Sufi teaching stories, "People" which looks at some historical and mythic figures, "Humor" which is more Sufi teaching stories, "Wisdom" that both looks at the use of various Sufi teaching modalities and provides more stories, "History, Whens And Wheres" which has a dozen or so pieces on historical eras from the earliest myths of Afghanistan up through the Mujahdin, and "The Red Bear From The North" which has stories of Afghani resistance to the Soviet invasion.

While all of this is good reading, the bit that stood out most for me was in the "Wisdom" section, in the "Wisdom of the Elephant" entry. In this Shah (Idries) discusses the famous "Elephant In The Dark"" story, but minutely picks apart the *intent* of the various levels of this sort of Sufi teaching vehicle. These three pages are the most direct statement of Sufi teaching structure that I can recall, and I've read *a lot* of books from Shah's various publishing entities over the years! Here's a little sample, where Shah is discussing *how* to view the stories:

> Remember, too, that in addition to analysis and discussion of written materials, there has to be perceptivity. The tales are not mechanical or preaching a belief. The are there to develop capacities in you. Let them seep into your mind.

Again, I can't recall a case where Shah has been *coaching* his readers like this ... that alone makes this a valuable book to have! Needless to say, I *highly* recommend getting a copy of Afghan Caravan[4]! This is entertaining, informative, and instructional, and could even be seen (despite the "conflict in Afghanistan" spin to a lot of it) as a very good introductory book to Sufi teachings (I know that I would have "absorbed" much of my reading over the years better had I read the above-noted section when first approaching this material!).

Of course, as an Octagon book, this is still in print, and both they and Amazon have it for $35.00 in hardcover. Oddly enough, there don't seem to be ANY used copies of the hardcover available via Amazon's "new/used" vendors, although you could get a used copy of the $19.00 paperback edition for around $11.00 ... but this is one that I'd say to "splurge" on and go buy the paperback at retail ~~(you might as well buy it direct from ISHK and give them Amazon's slice of the pie)! Poking around on the ISHK site, I see that this is also available (in hardcover) as part of a special package deal (much like the one I bought some time back), with four books for just $52.50 ($130.00 cover price), which is a pretty sweet deal (see HERE)~~. *{since this was published a decade ago, a lot of changes have happened over in ISHK and related sites, and I was currently unable to find this book, or the past several reviewed, anywhere over there ... although they are still available via Amazon}*.

Notes:

1. http://btripp-books.livejournal.com/21429.html
2-4. http://amzn.to/2cmWqfe

Tuesday, August 1, 2006[1]

And now for something completely different ...

Despite having worked in entrepreneurial settings for the past 30 years (my Mom's business, my own business, and my Wife's business), I've never been much of a "business guy" ... while being quite focused and dedicated to the work at hand, the "business of business" has never much interested me, and so I've never been one to seek out business seminars, magazines, or books. As such, Conor Cunneen's Why Ireland Never Invaded America[2] stands rather lonely in my library[3]; while it may not be the only "business book" in there, it certainly has precious little company. So, you might ask, how did I come to be reading this book?

Well, as followers of my main on-line journal know, I've been recently involved in yet another new job search, and have of late been rather obsessively attending things provided by Chicago's Career Transitions Center. Last Thursday, for the early morning session, Mr. Cunneen was the guest speaker, presenting his SHEIFGAB™[4] motivational structure to our group of desperate job seekers. Mr. Cunneen is an award-winning humorist and business speaker, and he very generously brought along copies of his book for all of us there that morning. Needless to say, I felt it would be *impolite* to not at least give the book a shot, and found that it was a bit of a confection (think peanut brittle), with nuggets of solid business advice set in a fast-reading humorous story.

As I have so little exposure to the "Corporate Strategy" genre, I can't "contextify" this as I might a book of Sufi stories, or an archaeological site survey, so let me get to "the facts". The book is "about" an Irish-American entrepreneur, Jake Boyd, who is on vacation visiting an Irish cousin (the inexplicably named Finbarr Kozlowski) back in "the old country" for a week's vacation. Jake's company has been struggling, and he's on the verge of throwing in the towel and selling it off. Finbarr, however, is constantly challenging him to look at things in new ways, and, in doing so, presenting 10 "corporate lessons", from the whimsical *Don't Believe Your Own Blarney* to such key elements as brand name, brand experience, and brand image. Having been an entrepreneur, there were many messages here that would have been quite useful in my previous businesses!

Why Ireland Never Invaded America[5] is available both via Amazon, etc., and from Cunneen's various inter-twined web sites[6] (it's amusing to me as a "web guy" how often you're in a different domain while navigating through his stuff ... although I don't think that's part of the *intentional* humor!). The book is also available via the new/used vendors, but I feel a bit churlish mentioning it, having been given a free signed copy. Anyway ... this is a fun read, with good "business lessons" ... if you're in the market for some easy-to-absorb marketing advice, this is one you should probably pick up!

Notes:
1. http://btripp-books.livejournal.com/21716.html
2. http://amzn.to/2bQV4ry
3. http://btripp-books.com
4. https://sheifgab.wordpress.com/
5. http://amzn.to/2bQV4ry
6. http://www.irishmanspeaks.com/

Wednesday, August 9, 2006[1]
A bit of a longer read ...

While not being an *uninteresting* read, I really don't have that much to say about Richard E.W. Adams' Prehistoric Mesoamerica[2], which probably has more to do with it being intended as a college textbook than anything else. This "revised edition" puts the chapters in a chronological order (where the original version started with the Aztecs, which was how the author preferred to teach the subject to his students), going from what pre-cultural archaeological traces there are in the region, into the Olmec, Mayan, etc., and up to the Spanish conquest.

As I've noted in a couple of reviews of late (on books on this subject), I somehow had mentally mis-placed Teotihuacan in time ... despite having spent quite a while there over several visits ... I had managed to peg it as far older than its 200-800 C.E. age, which has caused me to have to do some mental gymnastics to "deal with" the concept of it having had active inter-relations with various other mesoamerican cultures. Perhaps this is from my "buying into" the Aztec view that Teotihuacan was built by the Gods in some earlier epoch, rather than paying attention to dating information in the books and museums!

This comes up in relation to how Adams presents the cultures of the area as being much more interwoven (at least by trade) than is often pictured, with a lot more "fluidity" of ideas and alliances. In fact, for some regions, he argues that the "cultural definitions" of many groups are essentially arbitrary, being the result of anthropologists or archaeologists wanting to put a label on the "stuff in this valley" versus the "stuff in that valley".

The book is full of all sorts of interesting tidbits, such as the Tarascan culture having a language (and some architectural traits) that is related to the Quechua of the Incas in Peru and the language of the Zuni in the American southwest. However, this was hardly an "easy read", with way too many parts that read like this:

> *Internal motivations to cultural complexity may have been largely based on population growth. All indications are that during the Classic and Post-classic periods population increased and that elaborations of sociopolitical arrangements was one sign of increasing complexity.*

Although, to be fair, Adams does inject a wry humor to many observations, with comments like: *"the Tarascans themselves are still around to be consulted, at least on their language and other surviving matters of interest".*

Would I recommend Prehistoric Mesoamerica[3]? Sure, if you're interested in the subject to the extent that an in-depth analysis of it from a rather academic stance will hold your attention. There are a lot of maps, drawings and photos, but not so much that this would draw in the casual reader. The book does appear to be currently out of print, but can be had for under five bucks in "like new" condition from the Amazon used/new vendors (not bad, given its original $36.95 cover price).

Notes:

1. http://btripp-books.livejournal.com/21935.html
2-3. http://amzn.to/2blHURY

Friday, August 18, 2006[1]

Verrrry Interesting ...

So, I just passed my "finals" (an on-line written test and doing an oral hypnotic induction over the phone) and am now a "Certified Hypnotist" via the free on-line "Foundations of Hypnotherapy" course from the Hypnosis Motivation Institute (hypnosis.edu). I'd picked up this book (which is suggested for the course, but not required) to accompany that over the past month.

John G. Kappas, Ph.D. was the guy who "discovered" variable suggestibility in hypnosis, and this book, Professional Hypnotism Manual: A Practical Approach for Modern Times[2] introduces his modalities of "Physical and Emotional Suggestibility and Sexuality". Prior to Kappas' work, it was generally assumed that as much as 60% of the population "was not hypnotizable", but what he found was that the standard approaches to hypnotism only were targeted to a particular *type* of suggestibility (the "Physical"), and that with only minor (albeit significant) changes in wording and intonation, *everybody* could be hypnotized.

It's sort of telling that Dr. Kappas had come to hypnotism from a psychotherapy practice, as there is a lot in these theories which echo Freudian concerns. Kappas defines "Suggestibility" as arising in the child, though interactions with the primary caretaker (usually, the Mother), from birth to around 6. If the Mother presents congruent messages (follows through on punishments/rewards, fulfills promises, etc.), the child will become a Physical Suggestive, and will tend to respond to literal, direct communications ... however, if the Mother presents incongruent messages, the child will become an Emotional Suggestive, and will always be looking for the "hidden meaning" in things, and so will best respond to inferred or indirect communication. From about 6 to 9 the child is in a "socializing" phase where the influence of teachers, classmates, etc. begin to take effect. From ages 9 to 14 the child develops what Kappas calls their "Sexuality" (which, I believe, is an *unfortunate* choice of words, but is probably due to a Freudian background), which is more about how a person acts or prioritizes than about "sexuality" per se ... this is formed by emulating the secondary caretaker (the Father), with "Physical" resulting in priorities of "relationship/sex - children/family - hobbies - work", and "Emotional" resulting in priorities of "work - hobbies - family - sex". Again, while I think that the underlying dynamics of the Kappasian modalities are valid, I feel they'd be a LOT clearer had he applied different labels to them ... calling the "activity" dynamics "Sexuality" leads to all sorts of misconstrued assumptions about the hypnotherapy (although, to be fair, much of what Kaplan deals with in the "Sexuality" area *is* "relationship therapy", so there is a basis for this), and repeating the dichotomy of Physical vs. Emotional makes it very easy to create confusion! {n.b.: I found a site[3] that goes into much more of Kappas' theories that I care to here, in case you'd like to check that out!}

Anyway, I had been casting around for an "introduction to hypnosis" book when this free on-line training thing fell into my lap (and, by the way, the offer is still available[4] through the end of August), and certainly found this fascinating. The Professional Hypnotism Manual[5] is no "ooh, wow!" sort of book full of stage tricks or newage "when I was Cleopatra" claptrap, but a serious look at an approach to understanding people (in ways similar to a psychology book), and methods of reaching and helping them. While this *is* available from both Amazon and their new/used vendors (and, no doubt, from your local major bookstore), you're not getting much of a break from either (it's at full price at Amazon and the cheapest used one is just a few bucks less), so I'd suggest picking it up directly from the HMI bookstore[6] if this sounds like something you'd like to learn!

Notes:

1. http://btripp-books.livejournal.com/22041.html
2. http://amzn.to/2c0jEeE
3. http://www.durbinhypnosis.com/sugsex.htm
4. https://hypnosis.edu/distance/foundations/
5. http://amzn.to/2c0jEeE
6. http://www.hypnosis.edu/books/hypnotism-manual.asp

Sunday, August 20, 2006[1]

More straight talk ...

I was amazed at what a *difficult read* this Ann Coulter book was for me. While I had *loved* her preceding books Treason[2] and Slander[3], this one sort of blind-sided me. Perhaps this is due to both of those books being "exposés" of particular Leftist perfidies ... while this was a walk though recent history ... over much of which I'd managed to build up some emotional scar tissue.

As such, reading How to Talk to a Liberal (If You Must): The World According to Ann Coulter[4] was a bit like going to one of those awful post-accident physical therapy sessions where they pull apart the places where you've "healed wrong" so that the parts can end up where they're supposed to be. I found myself getting angry over and over and over again, as Ann opened up old psychic wounds. Not that I was getting mad *at her*, mind you ... but at the likes of the Klintons (and their various vile henchlings), the terror apologists, the execrable MSM, and all the "fellow travelers" of the Leftist ilk. I can't believe that I had nearly *forgotten* why I hated Bubba & Hitlery so much ... I guess having Islamofascists to worry about can make you remiss in watching your back against equally deadly enemies on the home front!

That being said, however, this is (like nearly all of Ann's books) "a breath of fresh air" in an all-too PC world. Ann is constantly manifesting the little kid that blurts out "but the Emperor has *no clothes*!", while throwing a gleefully harsh light on the willful lies, dark subterfuges, and evil intents of our "enemies foreign and domestic". I often worry that the history of our era will be written in the smarmy, duplicitous terms of the current media and educational cabals, and hope that somebody out there will create hundreds of "time capsules" in which to store Ann's books for future generations so that *one voice* of sanity might reach out and say "the Left destroyed everything of value, and it didn't used to be this way". Frankly, I wish that EVERY "liberal" would sit down and actually *read* Ann's books with the hope that some of them might come to have "a conversion experience" away from the neo-Stalinist sinkhole.

Of course, this brings me to my one quibble with Ms. Coulter. Christianity *"ain't all that and a bag of chips"*, honey! The fact that she has found a fairy-tale that makes her happy is *swell*, but the world does NOT necessarily come down to a Christian/moral-less dichotomy. One can be a moral, upstanding, name-your-virtue, human being without having to believe that a Universal Deity chose a particular tribe in a particular region of a particular planet out of all of creation for special blessings, and then embodied Itself into a hominid shell to "save" said special bipeds from some vaguely-defined mythological inherited transgressions (seriously, when you strip Christianity down to its key elements, it sounds more loony than the Heaven's Gate cult!). Not that her theological bias comes into play much in *this* book (unlike, as I understand it, her most recent volume[5]), it is an on-going "point of contention" that keeps me from becoming a 100% fawning fanboy.

All caveats aside, do pick up a copy of How to Talk to a Liberal (If You Must)[6] ... it is witty, insightful, caustic, brilliant, and exasperating ... and an unsubtle nudge to those of us in our "Right minds". This is, of course, still in print, so you could find it at your local bookstore ... Amazon, however, has it at ten bucks off of cover price at the moment, and their new/used vendors have "like new" copies for around five bucks ... a small price to pay for having one's eyes opened (again) to the twisted nature of our current world!

Notes:

1. http://btripp-books.livejournal.com/22459.html
2. http://btripp-books.livejournal.com/6772.html
3. http://btripp-books.livejournal.com/6510.html
4. http://amzn.to/2bZn2oo
5. http://amzn.to/2cwpkOh
6. http://amzn.to/2bZn2oo

Friday, August 25, 2006[1]

Whiiiiiiine ... now I want a VACATION!

As you can tell by the picture, this is not a pristine new copy of this book ... as much as I *theoretically* like used book sales/stores, I always get a bit "creeped out" by used books, especially if they're not "like new" and have a lot of traces of their previous owners. This is the first book I've read from my minor haul from the Newberry Library Book Fair last month, and it's certainly in the worst shape, having been obviously been heavily used (likely touring the ruins). Tikal: A Handbook of the Ancient Maya Ruins (with a guide Map)[2] by William R. Coe (currently missing its guide map), was a fascinating read, however. The 1975 seventh printing of Coe's 1967 book, this is a no-nonsense ruin-by-ruin look at the core of Tikal, from the interesting perspective of a researcher writing prior to the "deciphering" of the Mayan language (resulting in a lot of pictured, but untranslated glyphic inscriptions).

Now, I've traveled quite a bit to the Mayan sites in the Yucatan, but have never made it down to Tikal (which is in Guatemala), and I had *no idea* how massive the site is. The "central zone" alone covers around six square miles (with over 3,000 "constructions"), and Coe suggests that the city as a whole might spread out over something like 25 square miles! Tikal is also quite old, with over a millennia of what Coe describes as "apparently ceaseless" building, resulting in what he estimates as over 10,000 individual platforms or buildings lying beneath or within later construction in the central area alone! Unlike the later "sequenced" building as exhibited in such monuments as the *Castillo* at Chichen Itza (which was built over "bigger and better" at the start of every new 52-year calendar cycle), the residents of Tikal were in the habit of almost randomly tearing down old edifices and building new ones over-lying other parts of existing structures, resulting in what seems to be quite a confusion of buildings. The earliest layers of Tikal date to as early as 600 BCE, and there is a constant building and rebuilding of the city up to about 900 CE, when the lowland Maya civilization collapsed (in fact, there are several ruins which were abandoned mid-construction at that time). There are some really fascinating line drawings in this book which show the results of "trenching" down to the bedrock to reveal a vastly complicated series of over-laid development through that span of time.

I really need to do some research on the current state of "tourist Tikal" ... needless to say, in 1967, the logistics of visiting the ruins were rudimentary at best, but I'd guess that they've developed like the various Mexican sites, most of which have become much more "user friendly" even since I started to go down there! It's been over 10 years since I last did any "ruin travel" (The Wife was pregnant with our now 10-year-old Daughter #1 the last time we were down at Teotihuacan), and I sure miss it.

This book seems to be out of print (at least as far as Amazon, etc. are concerned), but I suspect it might still be available in Guatemala (the book is "officially" put out by the Museum of the University of Pennsylvania, but it was printed by one or more local publishers) ... not that this would help you in finding a copy! There *are* four or five versions listed on Amazon, but no available copies. If you run into it at a used book store or sale, do consider picking it up if you have an interest in Mayan archaeology, as it really is an interesting over-view of the site!

Notes:

1. http://btripp-books.livejournal.com/22560.html
2. http://amzn.to/2ckwctT

Friday, September 15, 2006[1]

Most recent book finished ...

Sometimes (like the past few weeks) I have long droughts where I don't finish any books, and then suddenly I'm boom-boom-boom with them. I really *do* try to schedule these better ... however, I just finished two books that I've been reading seemingly *forever* on back-to-back days. This is the review of the most recent one, skipping over another which I'm sort of still "processing"!

Anyway, A Forest of Kings: The Untold Story of the Ancient Maya[2], by Mayanists Linda Schele and David Freidel, is well known as a *classic* book on the subject. This had, however, sat around on my bookshelves since its publication in 1990 ... why, I don't know, really ... I just never quite got around to plowing into it. Perhaps the very "substantialness" of the book had put me off, as it is a rather dense slog at times, especially if one makes the effort of flipping back constantly to the 90 pages of endnotes which add an extra 20% to the length of the book (not even counting the 24 pages of *references* which follow!). What the authors have attempted is a start-to-finish *history* of the Mayan peoples (well, for the periods when there were Kings), based on the inscriptions and other archaeological traces that they left behind.

A Forest of Kings[3] was fascinating in being *full* of "I did not know that" moments, starting with its title. Most of the Mayan commemorative stele (like this fellow here[4]) were structured as symbolic representations of the King embodying "the World Tree" at the center of the Mayan cosmos, and so in sites with long habitation (where many of these, erected by successive generations of Kings, would fill a plaza) it would create "a forest" of Kings!

On several levels, though, this is an "odd" book. Most of it is *very* academic (with endless credits being detailed about other researchers who had previously suggested plausible theories that might support or disagree with the theories and/or assumptions that the authors were presenting, yadda, yadda, yadda), yet is interspersed with "stories" trying to flesh out moments in time and humanize the figures frozen in these stone carvings. It also is structured as a look at "Kingship" as an organizing concept in the Mayan world, from its first emergence in early sites through its eventual abandonment it late-period cultural expressions such as found at Chichen Itza. For most of Mayan history, the King was not just a political figure, but they main psychopompic actor of the state religion, responsible for *manifesting* (through personal rites of bloodletting and various forms of shamanic trance) various deities and ancestors. The ongoing patterns of inter-city warfare (frequently regulated by the movements of the planet Venus) are also detailed, as much of this was purely to provide "high status" captives whose abuse (some were kept alive for decades in order to be dragged out for ritual torture at important ceremonies) and/or execution played key roles in the prestige of Kings, nobles, and cities alike (yet also set up "blood feuds" that churned on for centuries between mutually hostile lineages).

As I've noted previously, it's only been in the past few decades that we've been able to *read* what the Mayan elites had inscribed of their history, so this bears (for me, at least, having been interested in the subject early on) much of the thrill of "new discovery" (even though the book's been out for sixteen years!).

Needless to say, I'd recommend this to anybody who has a serious interest in all things Mayan. It's not an *easy* book or a quick read, but it a very illuminating look into a world that was shrouded in mute mystery for a millennium. A Forest of Kings[5] appears to still be in print in a paperback reprint edition, so you should be able to find it at your local bookstore, but the Amazon new/used guys have it "like new" in paperback for as little as six bucks, and in hardcover for around nine. It's heavily illustrated with line drawings, and has a small 16-page section of color photos as well ... certainly a good addition to any archaeology fan's library.

Notes:

1. http://btripp-books.livejournal.com/23008.html
2-3. http://amzn.to/2blOx7S
4. https://goo.gl/tR43Do
5. http://amzn.to/2blOx7S

Tuesday, September 26, 2006[1]

Finally ...

I mentioned in my previous review[2] that I'd "skipped over" a book that I'd read, and it's been nearly two weeks and I figured I should get to this before I lose any sort of immediacy on the information. However, I still am not sure how to best approach Idries Shah's The Commanding Self[3] ... it presents a fairly unique quandary, I would really like to strongly recommend this, but on the other hand I feel that I would be doing readers a disservice in relation to the Sufi teaching material if this served as an introduction!

This is the last (as far as I know) of Shah's major works, and is the first one where he lets his readers "look under the hood" of the methods used in his style of Sufi teaching. Much of the book uses snippets from Q&A sessions and excerpts from various correspondences to correct misconceptions, answer a wide range of queries, and point out "blinders" that many people may have. Some sections are specifically this, others are stories, etc., that springboard off of these.

Again, what sets this apart from most of Shah's books is the direct look at the how/why of many Sufi teaching approaches. For instance (and the element which is, perhaps, most germane to my hesitancy in eagerly endorsing this book as an introduction to Sufi thought), at one point he answers a question as to why he doesn't put extensive explanatory sections in books such as the Nasrudin collections ... he indicates that these tales are designed to have a specific *effect* on the reader, which would be attenuated (if not eliminated) if they followed information "framing" them in their technical context.

This sort of "non-Sufi analysis" of materials that have a particular Sufi intent falls under the "irrelevant associations" which are half of what makes up the title function, the Commanding Self. Shah describes this mental pattern as a mixture of "primitive emotionalism" and these misconstrued attempts at analysis (based on habitual cultural or intellectual approaches which have nothing to do with the Sufi work). It is no doubt telling that the phrase ""The Commanding Self" sounds so *positive* to Western ears, and the fact that this pattern is something that we must *struggle against* (or at least struggle to be aware of its effects) is one of the subtler "teachings" of this book.

This being said, The Commanding Self[4] is a *remarkable* book, full of very to -the-point examinations of significant elements of the human experience. I found Shah's analysis of most religions especially enlightening ... for, as a rule, these are nothing but the "fossilized remnants" of what had one time been an active and specifically targeted teaching, now all wrapped up in the previously noted "primitive emotionalism" which provides nothing but a "conditioning function" ala modern techniques of brainwashing!

As many of my regular readers know, I've been having to be "quite thrifty" over the past few years, so it is saying something that I bought *two copies* of this book. I first ordered this in paperback from Amazon at their "retail" price (which was, admittedly, at a 30% discount from cover), but was so enamored of it that I bought a *hardcover* copy (from the new/used vendors) as well, to better go into my library. As the cliché goes ""no higher praise ..." than my voting with my much-conserved dollars!

Obviously, I am torn here, because part of me wants to insist that everybody reading this review immediately march out and pick up a copy of The Commanding Self[5], because it is *that important*, yet another side of me wants to be responsible (if somewhat unrealistic) and encourage you to read a dozen or so *other* of Shah's books *first* and *then* delve into this one! As I have read somewhere upwards of fifty books by Shah, his various associates (and pseudonyms), and the output of his several research and publishing ventures, I came to this book with substantial context for what he presents here ... others (going by the Amazon reviews) don't have this perspective and have called this book "judgmental" and "egomaniacal". I worry that if folks come to this book *first* they will come away with similar ill-considered impressions.

Anyway, in closing, let me say that it has been a *long time* since I got quite such a kick in the pants from a book as I've had from The Commanding Self[6]. It may open up whole new vistas of perception for you, or it might turn you off of Sufism altogether. I, at least, am sure to be re-reading this a number of times (again, high praise from me). Like nearly all Octagon books, this is still in print, and is available from ~~ISHK (or Octagon if in the UK)~~ *{due to changes since this review was initially published, try* here[7]*}* directly , as well at a discount from Amazon, and (in hardcover) as little as $6.15 from their new/used vendors. I guess I'll just have to say "do what thou wilt" (and all that) in regards to this one!

Notes:

1. http://btripp-books.livejournal.com/23089.html
2. http://btripp-books.livejournal.com/23008.html
3-6. http://amzn.to/2cw5GBT
7. http://idriesshahfoundation.org/books/the-commanding-self/

Thursday, September 28, 2006[1]

Skipping ahead again ...

You know, I would *really* prefer it if my reviews here followed along with my finishing books, but I've been hitting a few that I've needed more time to get around to reviewing, right about the same time that I hit others that I'm able to simply spew out an opinion. This is one of those cases. If you want to check the actual reading order, you can always visit my LibraryThing catalog[2], of course.

I realize that frequently my "book reviews" are more about my reaction to a book than a specific analysis of the book itself, and I'm afraid that this one is going to be very much and example of this tendency. First of all, I have to admit that I have never read the very popular book *The Prophet* by Kahlil Gibran which is the inspiration for Gunther Schaule's The Prophet Returns[3]. The back cover copy refers to this as a "sequel", but I have a strong suspicion that a better category description would be "fanfic", as I can't imagine that a book that has sold over a million copies (the original *The Prophet*) is as weak as this seemed to me. Again, having not read Gibran's book, I have no way of knowing if it, too, was simply a treacly bit of newage woo-woo that appealed to a lot of people looking for emotional stimulation, or if it actually is a vehicle for insights of some depth.

This book took an odd route into my library, being a "sample" sent out by a print-on-demand place that I was looking at in the days when I was trying to find ways of saving Eschaton (my old publishing company, for those coming in late). It has been sitting around in various piles of stuff for many years, and recently got "reorganized" into an actual stack of books and caught my eye when I was looking for a "quick read" (it's only like 100 pages) this week to "buffer" the order of other things I'm reading (*"it's an OCD thing, you wouldn't understand"*). So, this is a book that I didn't actually intend to own, based on another book that I've not read, so my connection with it is at best at some cognitive distance!

I assume that the "parable-like" style of the writing is intended to sound like Gibran's, so I'll give that a pass ... however the main character is constantly talking about his studies at the Library of Alexandria, yet then interjecting commentary about "alcohol and drugs" or concepts derived from modern astrophysics. If Schaule wants to make this an "ancient tale", at least keep the references in the right millennia! Schaule seems to have written this as a way of "revealing" some wisdom from his own head, which appears to be his "six pillars" (work, family, society and body, mind, spirit) model, which is hardly news to anybody even vaguely familiar with even *popular* metaphysical traditions. Aside from the out-of-time incongruities, there are also many *strongly implausible* "plot twists" that seem simply to be ways of interjecting a few other secondary points, and most irritating of all was the closing allusions which tie the whole story into the Christian mythos (*spoiler:* the main characters are Mary's parents).

Back in the day, I saw a lot of manuscripts like this come in from people who thought they had Real Important Things To Say. Of course, back then it was quite an undertaking to self-publish ... The Prophet Returns[4] is a prime example of the *downside* of how easy it is to get a book printed these days! This Schaule fellow seems to have a telephone business down in Australia that allows him to run his (oh, OK, I'll say it) *vanity press* on the side, and I'm sure it makes him feel like an Enlightened Spiritual Being (™) to have this book in circulation.

Oddly enough, this is available from Amazon (although they say it takes 4-6 *weeks* to fill an order, so I guess they have to be shipped from Australia first) and its new/used vendors. Frankly, I couldn't imagine why somebody would want to buy this (unless, I suppose, if one was a big *The Prophet* junkie and wanted to get anything associated with that), but it will run you $8.95 new and around three bucks used if you were so inexplicably inclined.

Notes:

1. http://btripp-books.livejournal.com/23456.html
2. http://btripp-books.com
3-4. http://amzn.to/2cw5WRd

Saturday, September 30, 2006[1]

Catching up ...

This was another one which was "hard to write about", but for different reasons. What Survives?: Contemporary Explorations of Life After Death[2] (edited by Gary Doore), is an *interesting* book, but, by its very nature, *uneven*. This comprises a collection of 20 papers more-or-less on the title theme, assembled under four major headings: "The Evidence for Survival", "The Challenge of Materialism", "Death and Beyond in the Perennial Philosophy", and "Transcendence of Death". Many "leading lights" of modern new-age thought lend their words ... Ken Wilber, Colin Wilson, Stanley Krippner, Rupert Sheldrake, even Ram Dass ... each with a different stance, pacing, and style, making some parts of the book flow effortlessly, and others drag on. Needless to say, the subjects of the various papers also ranged all over the board, from looks at studies of reincarnation reports, to philosophical over-views on death, to shamanic systems, to a step-by-step look at the Tibetan *Bardo* teachings, to reports of hospice workers, to NDE reports, to the "usual suspects" new age theorizings bent to at least touch on the theme of the book.

I found parts of this *fascinating* and extremely thought-provoking (especially in relation to the fairly recent loss of my Mother), and others *tiresome* ... but I guess that could be expected from having 20 approaches to the subject strung together like this. I was somewhat disappointed that there wasn't a section of "dissenting voices", the "Challenge of Materialism" part was comprised of *responses* to the materialistic stance, and not a representation of that view ... however, I suspect that the Tarcher folks decided that would only irritate their target audience!

This is yet another volume that has been sitting around on my to-be-read shelves since the early 90's, but it seems less dated than many of those. There was plenty here to keep my head busy with "compare and contrast" churning (especially in relation to stuff like the remarkable Zen Physics[3] or some of the books on multi-dimensional cosmologies, etc.) here, although I couldn't say I particularly *enjoyed* the read.

As such, I can only give a tepid recommendation for What Survives?[4] ... if you have a particular fascination/interest in "death issues", this would certainly be a good book to add to your mental storehouse, but unless you are particularly looking for things along this line, I'd give it a pass. Like many of my "stale" books, this seems to be out of print, but is available via the Amazon new/used vendors for as little as a buck used, and nine bucks "new". If you're looking for a wide spectrum of views on possible survival of death, this is worthwhile, but it's hardly a "page turner" for the average reader.

Notes:
1. http://btripp-books.livejournal.com/23793.html
2. http://amzn.to/2bQdwAC
3. http://btripp-books.livejournal.com/7525.html
4. http://amzn.to/2bQdwAC

Thursday, October 5, 2006[1]

Hyperspace ...

Here's another of those "been sitting around a bit too long on my to-be-read shelves" books. This dates to the early 90's, and it really *hurts* to read physics writers *gushing* about "how exciting things will be when the SSC comes on-line". Of course, the Superconducting Super Collider got killed back in 1993 (this book, which came out in 1994, must have been finished just before that happened) when Clinton had his new Energy czar pull the plug on the funding. Admittedly, this is just one factor of this (and similar books), but it's one of those things that reminds me that letting stuff like this "age" too long before reading is not the optimal approach!

I suppose that it's not too much of an exaggeration to say that this book has become something of a "classic" ... it's still available in hardcover a dozen years down the road from publication, and goes for $40 on Amazon (the paperback can be had for a lot less). In Hyperspace: A Scientific Odyssey through Parallel Universes, Time Warps, and the Tenth Dimension[2] Michio Kaku looks at the cutting edge of cosmology, sketches out the history of how we got here, and does some projecting into the future.

One of the key elements here is, obviously, the concept of multi-dimensionality, which is often a hard thing to wrap one's brain around. Relying on the classic "flatland" examples (of how beings in a 2-D world would perceive 3-D objects), Kaku shows how, as odd as they seem, higher-dimension models go a long way towards explaining "issues" with many of the other theories. Most of this has to do with mathematics, and I'm not going to try to explain any of that here, but suffice it to say, stuff that "looks wrong" in the Standard Model suddenly "fits" if one posits a 10-dimensional (or 26-dimensional) universe. In fact, many of the "problems" with the vast proliferation of subatomic particles could also be explained as being expressions of a few specific things in differing harmonics (or something like that).

Oddly enough, a version of the multi-dimension theory had been popular in the 1800's, and was embraced by various Theosophists and the "spiritual research" folks of the day (many of whom also held prestigious university science chairs). This is part of the reason why it took such a long time to come back to it (as it had become the province of séances, rather than the laboratory). Indeed, Kaku holds that we wouldn't have this theory *now* if not for the brief, and almost lost, mathematical career of the prodigy Srinivasa Ramanujan (who died in his 30's), which he describes as "injecting 21st-century physics" into our current models.

Kaku also looks to the future (and helps explain why we've not had confirmable contacts with alien civilizations) by using Nikolai Kardashev's "Type I, Type II, Type III" civilization model. Kaku points out that we're currently in a "Type 0" civilization, and suggests that the stresses involved in this phase (conflicting nation-states with nuclear weapons and limited natural resources) are quite likely to result in a collapse of the civilization before it can reach beyond its home world. Frankly, in this model it appears that one *cannot* move from a "Type 0" to a "Type I" without having a "winner" that imposes its culture over the whole civilization ... a thing to consider when one thinks of current global politics! Even more concerning is his observation that whatever beings do end up successfully reaching a "Type I" civilization, they will almost certainly be evolved from high-functioning *predators* in their environment, and are not likely to be cute and cuddly ETs ... leading to the supposition that the interactions with them would likely more resemble the Spanish in Tenochtitlan than any newage vision of "enlightened beings".

Anyway, if you have an interest in these sorts of things, you should definitely pick up a copy of Hyperspace[3]. As noted above, it's still in print, so should be available at your local bookstore, as well as on-line. You can get a "like new" version of the hardcover edition for under six bucks (and a "very good" copy for under $2), and Amazon has the paperback on-sale for just under $11.00 ... so it shouldn't break the bank to check this out if it piques your curiosity.

Notes:

1. http://btripp-books.livejournal.com/23838.html

2-3. http://amzn.to/2bMOGle

Saturday, October 14, 2006[1]

Castaneda ...

I'm getting so *bad* ... I used to dive right in to writing these reviews when I finished the book, now, you never know. I finished reading this a week ago, and am only getting off my duff to write about it because I'm within a couple of hours of reading of finishing up a follow-up similarly-themed book!

This is not to say I've been *avoiding* the subject ... The Power of Silence: Further Lessons of Don Juan[2] was quite interesting ... it's just "what can you say about" a book by Carlos Castaneda? I'd read his "classic" first five books back in the 1970's, and they were certainly a significant factor in my subsequent Shamanic studies (although the work of the Peruvian Shamans with whom I've studied differed greatly from the "don Juan" model) ... and have since caught up with a couple of more.

If you're not familiar with Castaneda's books, they deal with his contacts with a Yaqui Shaman by the name of don Juan Matus ... Castaneda starts out as an earnest anthropologist and ends up as a Nagual. There is much conflicting opinion on the veracity of these stories, but it is very difficult for an outsider to judge ... there is a base-line consistency in the "mythos", however, which leads me to believe that these are, in fact, actual transmissions of a particular tradition (often referred to as "Toltec").

What is most interesting in The Power of Silence[3] is the information on don Juan's "lineage", with stories about his teacher and his teacher's teacher, along with background on how don Juan was trained. In fact, a substantial part of this book is don Juan spinning these sorts of stories. There are other elements which involve Castaneda (including some fascinating stuff about not being able to remember *really important information* that one has learned in altered perceptions), but this is largely a book about the different styles and personalities and approaches of these shamanic teachers.

This is available in a paperback reissue edition, so you should be able to find it in your local store, but you can snag a copy of the hardcover from Amazon's new/used vendors for as little as two bucks (and can get a "like new" copy for under seven). Would I recommend this to somebody who hadn't read much in the genre? I don't know ... it could be confusing without the in-depth context the other books provide. However, if you read his early books and hadn't caught the later ones, this provides a very valuable look into a different area of the knowledge.

Notes:

1. http://btripp-books.livejournal.com/24072.html
2-3. http://amzn.to/2bMMABQ

Monday, October 16, 2006[1]

Wish there were more books like this ...

I don't know off-hand if I've ever picked up a book with quite this format. Victor Sanchez's The Teachings of Don Carlos: Practical Applications of the Works of Carlos Castaneda[2] is an attempt at extracting the actual *exercises* detailed in the Castaneda books into something like a *manual*. Needless to say, there are dozens of teachers whose materials would benefit from this sort of attention!

Now, Victor Sanchez is hardly a "disinterested observer" (being that he has his own series of courses and workshops), but, having at least been in personal contact with Castaneda (it is unclear whether Sanchez "studied" with him or not, or simply had interviews/conversations on assorted topics), he's in a good position to package the materials up like this.

Whether the "donjuanist" material really lends itself to this approach is another question. This is hardly like Serge King's *Urban Shaman* which has exercises and workings that nearly anybody could do in the context of their daily lives. Much of what Sanchez details here requires significant access to isolated natural settings, and many things are structured to take several months of dedicated work. That is not to say that there aren't *immediately useful* exercises and instructions in the book, for there are (such as types of breathing, dream work, etc.), but the "take away" I had was that most of this work was for folks who could afford to take off a year and run away to the desert.

Frankly, I was disappointed that there weren't clear instructions for "working with the Assemblage Point", which seems to be such a key element in the Castaneda books. Over the years I have done quite a lot of Shamanic "energy work" and, while having a pretty good fix on most of the other "energetic" descriptions in the material, am still unclear, from an *activity* standpoint, what exactly don Juan means by the "Assemblage Point" and what is involved in *shifting* it. I had hoped that this book would address this central concept, but it seems to skim past it into materials that are, perhaps, more central to *Sanchez's* work.

Despite these caveats, this is a very useful book. Aside from the main part (which is "concept descriptions" coupled with exercises), there is a glossary of techniques which references particular page numbers in the various Castaneda book, making it fairly easy for one to go back to the source material even when this is spread out over several volumes.

The Teachings of Don Carlos[3] is still in print, so should be available from your local stores, but can also be had for under two bucks *new* from the Amazon new/used vendors. If you've read several of the Castaneda books, you might well consider adding this to the mix ... I just wish there were more book following this approach out there for *other* metaphysical traditions!

Notes:
1. http://btripp-books.livejournal.com/24516.html   2-3. http://amzn.to/2bMLTbJ

Monday, October 30, 2006[1]

Wow ...

Not being a reader of *fiction*, I rarely run into a "can't put it down" book ... frankly, I'm more likely to be taking a month to plow through some physics tome than to rip through a book in a day, but that's what I did with this one!

And, this is *quite* a book ... unfortunately, upon finishing it, I have pretty much the same reaction that I had when finishing Adventures in Afghanistan[2] ... it's something that I *really wish* was real, but I deeply suspect is some fictional yarn spun out for purposes of delivering veiled teachings. This too reels the reader in with fantastic events, hovering on the edge of plausibility just enough that one is willing to suspend a degree of disbelief as one is reading, but by the end the sheer volume of unlikely events leads one to pull back and wonder what was actually the point of the tale.

Alvin Schwartz's An Unlikely Prophet: A Metaphysical Memoir by the Legendary Writer of Superman and Batman[3] is (as one could gather from the sub-title) structured as a memoir of one of the leading lights of "the Golden Age of comics". Schwartz was 80 when he first wrote this ten years ago, but he was apparently still extant for this 2006 re-issue, as evidenced by both the included biographical info *and* the signature I found on the cover page (I don't know if the Amazon "new/used" vendor realized they had a *signed* copy when they sold it for a buck-eighty five!), and seems to be driven to deliver a particular "message" with this book (the previous edition bore the far more metaphysical sub-title *"Revelations on the Path without Form"*, which seems to have been abandoned to reach a wider audience).

The premise here is, by any gauge, *fantastic* ... that Schwartz, at age 80, is contacted by a mysterious (and *7ft tall*) stranger who claims to be a Tibetan *tulpa*, a mind-generated entity that takes physical form, who tells Schwartz that his Superman character is a part-formed *tulpa* as well. The book is pretty much Schwartz trying to figure out What This All Means. There is a certain dream-like quality to the narrative, with continuity holes that one could drive the proverbial truck through, but it *does* seem anchored in some fairly solid theory. Time and again I found concepts (and sources) mentioned that I'd previously encountered in my own Vajrayana studies, plus a good deal of reference to fairly recent scientific writings (that I'd likewise also read), and *dynamic* elements dealing with disincarnate zones which were very familiar from my Shamanic work (I found it interesting how often what Schwartz was writing paralleled techniques that Castaneda wrote about). This, of course, could mean as little as the author and I having very similar reading habits, but I found it *interesting* that this seemed to be tied in with so many areas in which I was at least conversant.

Perhaps it was this familiarity that made this book so engrossing for me ... although it certainly had other things in it that were enticing (like his stories of living next to Jackson Pollock, and various literary figures that he knew over the years). Needless to say, it was a *quick read*. The red flags that went up for me, however, came in the final chapters where *others* (his wife, his agent, etc.) suddenly were opening up about how they had previously unrevealed "secrets" that dove-tailed in with the events in Schwartz's main story line ... it just got too tidy on that level, while being somewhat dismissive with the actual *tulpa* (within *days* of the "climactic events" the house where the *tulpa* had lived had new residents, etc., which lends more to the "dreamlike" feel and less to the story's plausibility).

Schwartz's "The Path Without Form" (what seems to be the key element he's seeking to communicate here), deals primarily with the "I identification" and how it can be manipulated and brought to bear in various situations. I just wish he'd taken the extra step of moving out of the "fictionalized narrative" of the memoir format to throw in a "theory & practice" chapter at the end! Again, much of the *details* dealt with in the book are based on "real stuff", and much of the "experiential" descriptions ring true enough to one who has done a certain amount of "work" in these areas.

An Unlikely Prophet[4], having just been re-released this year, is still available at bookstores and via Amazon, etc. but can be found for as little as six bucks (sorry, no deals like the one I got!) via the "new/used" vendors.

Notes:

1. http://btripp-books.livejournal.com/24649.html
2. http://btripp-books.livejournal.com/20618.html
3-4. http://amzn.to/2ciWrnb

Saturday, November 4, 2006[1]

Another recent read ...

Ah, once again I jumped out-of-order on doing these reviews. I've had this one sitting around for a while, trying to figure out exactly what angle to take on it, but figured I'd just as well plow into doing the review (while it was reasonably fresh in my mind), rather than waiting for the ideal inspiration.

Mihaly Csikszentmihalyi's (and, no, I don't have *clue* how that's pronounced!) Flow: The Psychology of Optimal Experience[2] is, I take it, something of "a classic" at this point and has been the basis of several derivative books on the subject. Based on Csikszentmihalyi's continuing research, it looks at how some people are able to exist quite contentedly in the most stressful/meager situations, while others are miserable in lives of ease and plenty, and tries to get to the psychological "why" behind this. This examination comes from various angles, from the "contentedness" of hard-working pastoral villages to the array of experiences exhibited by urban factory workers, and from the rather counter-intuitive reality that most modern people get more satisfaction (are in more "flow") at work than they are in their leisure hours.

Of course, the whole concept of "flow" is a bit amorphous ... although it is a state that we all recognize and appreciate when it happens. Perhaps most culturally identified with sports, it's that point where everything that we're doing is *working* towards attaining our goals in a seemingly seamless web of interacting elements. Csikszentmihalyi breaks this down as an interface of challenges and skills, with an ideal zone being where our skills are extended to meet our challenges ... too little challenge, an there is boredom, too little skill and there is anxiety.

Pretty much "the answer" is breaking things down into manageable, achievable, step-by-step goals ... as long as one is having small successes (which have *some* challenge to them), one is likely to be happy in one's activities. Mental control also feeds into this, as does paying attention to how one spends one's time (i.e., avoiding TV).

Anyway, Flow[3] is still in print in a re-print edition, so you should be able to find it via your local bookstore, but the Amazon new/used vendors have it for as little as a couple of bucks.

Notes:

1. http://btripp-books.livejournal.com/25086.html
2-3. http://amzn.to/1dpeWC4

Sunday, November 5, 2006[1]

More shamanic stuff ...

Got done reading this one today, and figured that I'd try to crank out a review before the details started to slip away. When I'd read those other Castaneda book a while back I'd checked into what I did or did not have and picked up the missing books from the Amazon new/used vendors. As I'd noted previously, I'd read the first five Castaneda books back in the 70's and hadn't noticed until recently that there had been several new books out since.

Carlos Castaneda's The Eagle's Gift[2] seems to be the sixth book, although it followed several years past the initial five. This is structured differently from its predecessors (at least as I'm able to recall) in that Castaneda isn't working directly with Don Juan, but with his extended group, and the over-all course of the book is "tidying up things" as Don Juan and his associates prepare to "leave the world", a process which initially sounds like he's *dying* but actually is a major metaphysical undertaking involving a conceptualization of power called "The Eagle", which I don't pretend to really understand.

Towards the end of this book, Castaneda describes Don Juan speaking with each of his group individually, making sure that all are clear on the various aspects of their workings. On one level, this seems to be the point of The Eagle's Gift[3], as parts go through various aspects of *dreaming*, parts go though various aspects of *stalking*, and parts deal with the details of the structure of a "Warrior group"", and how this relates to something called "the rule".

I know that it sounds like a huge cop-out, but much of the details have already slipped from my recall ... however, in the book it repeatedly notes that it is *typical* that the interactions with things in non-normal reality are quickly forgotten by the part of the mind which operates within normative reality ... frankly, much of the book deals with Castaneda trying to re-connect with stuff that he didn't know he did/learned/knew from various experiences, so I guess I'm in good company in my "forgetting"!

That said, the details are still in the book (yeah, and I suppose I *could* go through with note cards and *research* this, but I'm not going to at the moment), which makes it quite a good reference for the "Yaqui" (or what has more recently been re-packaged as "Toltec") methodologies framed as *dreaming*, *stalking*, etc. The fact that Don Juan, etc., (in a mundane temporal sense) exit the story line at this point, also make this something of the pivot-point between the "classic" first five, and the later works (often seen as being less "legitimate" or tradition-based than the original material).

It appears that this is still available in a paperback reprint edition, so you should be able to find a copy at your local bookstore, but I picked up the hardcover from the Amazon new/used vendors, and you can still get a "very good" condition copy there for around two bucks (plus shipping) if this sounds like it needs to be in *your* library too!

Notes:
1. http://btripp-books.livejournal.com/25256.html
2-3. http://amzn.to/2bDDJ8a

Wednesday, November 15, 2006[1]

Another good one ...

Well, I'm glad that I followed up Carlos Castaneda's The Eagle's Gift[2] with The Fire from Within[3], as they really could be seen as "paired" books, detailing two accounts of Castaneda's last year or so with Don Juan. As I noted in my review for the former, that covered the activities with the rest of Castaneda's "Warrior group", and led up to Don Juan (and the others of that group) making some strange metaphysical departure into other realms. Well, *this* book deals with Castaneda's activities with Don Juan during the same period, with some of these (most notably, the dramatic last test) referred to in the other.

This is, perhaps, more "technical" than some of the other books, as Don Juan spends much of the book trying to get Carlos "up to speed" as the new Nagual, putting him through various exercises to shift his "assemblage point" and move through various levels of existence as needed, in preparation for such time that he'd be on his own. The main test at the end (referenced in the previous book) is Castaneda and a couple of the other warriors of his party having to *jump off a mountain cliff* "into an abyss", the test being, of course, in that they must *bodily* shift into an alternative reality to avoid being killed by the fall (all of them survive).

Again, having studied some analogous traditions, I find the details of these things *fascinating*, and there is quite a lot to absorb along these lines in both of these books. This one also gives yet another version of Don Juan's teacher, the Nagual Julian, from Don Juan's perspective, as opposed to the story told Castaneda in the earlier book. Don Juan also discusses how their lineage developed, based on the ancient sorcerers (the "Toltecs", one of whom, a "death defier" was still actively linked to them), but diverging into a new understanding.

I was also quite interested in something that dove-tailed with other traditions about "God", such as that dealing with Metatron ... in this Don Juan insists that what humans see as "God" in mystical, spiritual, and religious experiences is simply "the Mold of Man", the *template* (somewhat ala one of Sheldrake's morphogenetic fields) which assembles us on this plane. An "emanation of the Eagle", it is perceived by seers as divine, but is simply the "perfected image" of our own state of being ...."*the mold is our God because we are what it stamps us with and not because it has created us from nothing and made us in its image and likeness*" ... it is simply human self-centeredness that dresses this up in the trappings we've invented for divinity and calls it "God".

The problem with being the seventh book in a series, is that (to a greater or lesser extent), the book is necessarily based on its predecessors. While I, having had read all the previous books at various points (and studied similar traditions), can "get" much of what is going on in The Fire from Within[4] ... and while I would love to heartily recommend this and *The Eagle's Gift* ...

that rave has to come with caveats that a reader unfamiliar with the "Castaneda universe" is likely to have a hard time in absorbing what's going on. That said, this *is* a rather remarkable book, and I'm certainly glad to have it in my collection! Again, this is still in print, so you should be able to find a copy at your local book store, but you can find it in the hardcover edition (what I picked up) for under a buck via the Amazon new/used vendors.

Notes:

1. http://btripp-books.livejournal.com/25515.html
2. http://btripp-books.livejournal.com/25256.html
3-4. http://amzn.to/2cd3Z8c

Friday, November 24, 2006[1]

Catching up ...

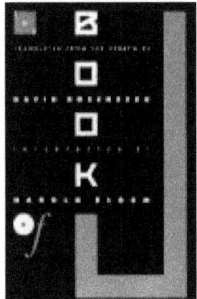

This is another of those books that I've had sitting around for a few days, not quite able to "pull the trigger" on writing a review. Oh, well. I just got done with *another* book, which I'd been slogging through for nearly two months, and figured I should get this one up before I ended up with a growing backlog of things to write about!

The Book of J[2] was one of those things that I just stumbled over (in this case, at the Newberry Library Book Fair ... a hardcover *signed copy* for two bucks!) and decided to pick up, and then for no particular reason opted to slot it into my reading schedule (it was "something different" from what I'd been reading, so was somewhat functioning as "mental floss"). It's sort of an odd book ... it's "interpreted by" Harold Bloom based on the translation of David Rosenberg ... but is essentially a book of Biblical exegesis, looking at the "J" author of substantial bits of the Old Testament. Now, as a former Religion Major, I am at least conversant with the analytical dissection of various ancient texts, but was not specifically up to speed on this particular area. It seems that "J" is the extracted source of many of the classic Bible stories, as opposed to "E", "P", "D", or "R" who were other writers/schools that either added materials, edited out materials, re-organ-ized materials, or otherwise spun a collection of bronze-age tribal myths into the document which has inexplicably held sway over vast chunks of humanity over the past couple of millennia.

Bloom (whose own writing in remarkably well crafted, I found myself marveling over many phrases and wondering just how long it took him to come up with such stellar prose!), posits that "J" was writing in the court of Solomon, perhaps in the days of Rehoboam, and that (from various thematic clues) *she* was a noble lady of the court. Bloom compares her to Shakespeare, Chaucer, and even to later authors such as Kafka, pointing to the ironic stance emblematic to the "J" material. The God of the "J" material is hardly the deity envisioned by most Christians or Muslims (or for that matter, most Jews), as He is a being who eats, rests, walks, and *argues* with His chosen creations. This God also appears to manifest behaviors that would be, in a human, regarded and psychologically unstable ... but these "quirks" are simply noted, ironically, and not questioned in the "J" material.

The book is basically in three parts, the first section where Bloom puts forth his reasoning about "J" and provides more info on the times and the location, a central section which is Rosenberg's (who, I take it, seems to be a noted Hebrew poet) translation of the extracted "J" material, and a final section where Bloom walks us through the story, highlighting major characters. This is fairly interesting stuff (especially *for Biblical exegesis*), and, as I noted previously, quite well written.

<u>The Book of J</u>[3] appears to still be in print in a paperback edition, so should be reasonably easy to find if you were so inclined. However, you can pick up a "like new" copy from the Amazon new/used vendors for as little as a penny, so there is that as an alternative. Again, I don't know how interested "most folks" would be in this volume ... but if picking apart a puzzle based on ancient texts is your thing, this would probably work for you.

Notes:

1. http://btripp-books.livejournal.com/25815.html
2-3. http://amzn.to/2cd4q24

Sunday, November 26, 2006[1]

An unusually long read ...

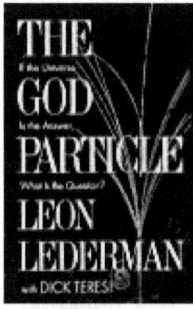

Well, *that* was an odd one ... I started reading this right after knocking down Michio Kaku's Hyperspace[2] back at the beginning of October, meaning that I was "stuck in it" for over 7 weeks! What's strange about this is that the book is neither excessively long (400-some pages), or dully-written, or overly technical. Quite to the contrary, Nobel laureate Leon Lederman (or his co-author Dick Teresi) keeps The God Particle: If the Universe Is the Answer, What Is the Question?[3] quite engaging throughout, but for some reason I ended up making *very* slow progress through it.

Now, some would say "Hey, it's a *physics* books, what do you expect?", but I *like* physics books, especially ones using as much humor as is in this one. Lederman takes an interesting approach here, looking at the entire "intellectual history" of the search for the foundation particles of the world, from Democritus' "a-toms" to the products of the current massive colliders, discussing the evolution of the theories and how they related to discoveries from the lab (Lederman, being an "experimentalist" makes many jibes at the "theoretical" side of the physics department). Unfortunately, this is yet another book written *before* Clinton pulled the plug on the SSC (although it's not as unrestrained as Kaku in its enthusiasm, it seems that Lederman knew that the SSC was in serious jeopardy from the new regime in 1992), so it does have some of that "breathless anticipation" of all these cool new discoveries that seemed to be just around the corner in the Bush 1 era.

So, what's this "God Particle"? Well, it takes Lederman 340 pages to get around to that. Surprise! (or not, to science readers or fans of the Lexx[4] TV series) It's the much-written of "Higgs Boson". Why is the Higgs boson the "God Particle"? It embarrasses me to say I'm not sure ... though it does seem to be one of those "missing links" (I was going to say "along with the Top/Truth quark" but I just noticed[5] that this was discovered last year!) that would allow for a nice pat "Theory of Everything" with tidy symmetries from the innards of hadrons up through macro-world effects like electro-magnetism. It probably has something to do with being a quanta associated with the "Higgs field" which, in theory, permeates every place in the universe at all times, and *gives mass to all particles* (which, I assume, eventually points to a way of merging gravity into the Standard Model), but I could be off on that.

Anyway, The God Particle[6] *is* (despite my long drag through it), a very informative and entertaining book (if, of course, you like science). This does seem to still be in print via a paperback reprint edition, so ought to be available through your local bookseller, but you could also snag a "very good" copy of the hardcover for under a buck via the Amazon new/used vendors!

Notes:
1. http://btripp-books.livejournal.com/25930.html
2. http://btripp-books.livejournal.com/23838.html
3. http://amzn.to/2bDAwp4
4. http://en.wikipedia.org/wiki/Lexx
5. http://en.wikipedia.org/wiki/Top_quark
6. http://amzn.to/2bDAwp4

Tuesday, November 28, 2006[1]

I should have read this 25 years ago ...

Well, poking around on my shelves for "what to read next" I hit a stack of books which either date to or right after the Kalachakra Initiation that His Holiness gave in New York City (at Madison Square Garden, of all places) back in 1991. I don't recall if I bought these books on-site, or if I ordered them afterward, but there are like a half-dozen various titles (still) waiting for me to get around to reading them.

The Opening of the Wisdom Eye[2] by Tenzin Gyatso, the 14th Dalai Lama, was not what I expected. Not that I had a specific idea of what this was about (I was thinking it might have to do with visualization exercises, the type that are central to Vajrayana practices like the Kalachakra), but I really didn't expect this to be something of a "Tibetan Buddhist primer". It turns out that this is a re-print of a book that H.H. wrote back in 1963 (translated to English in 1966) which was intended as *"a clear and comprehensive introduction to the teachings of the Buddha"*. I'm not sure that the book actually achieves that goal, at least for Western readers, though ... it struck me as more a volume on "how Tibetan Buddhism (and especially Vajrayana) fits into the over-all Buddhist world" as H.H. puts quite a lot of focus into framing Vajrayana as part of a continuum from basic Theraveda practices on through the very complex exercises of his own lineage.

When I say that I don't feel that this book achieves clarity, it's because this is, to a certain extent, a *technical manual* and it seems to assume a certain level of pre-existing knowledge on the part of the reader. Now, I have read quite a lot of Tibetan Buddhist material over the past few decades, but have not *practiced* this in any more than the most cursory fashion (I've worked intensely with certain developmental exercises, but have not worked with the material in any systematic form), and there are *substantial* parts of this book that have me scratching my head and going "oh, uh, yeah ... OK". To randomly pick out an example of this, in the "Training In Supreme Collectedness" section (part of "The Threefold Training" part of the book), there are the Nine States of Mind, the Six Powers, and the Four Mental Activities. Of the latter, #1 is *"1. Manonivesapravartak-manaskara - By means of this activity the mind enters into the object."* ... that's *it*, not defining terms, not contextifying action, just the statement as it is. Now, I'm not asking for some Klintonesque "definition of *is*", but it would be nice to have some commentary about what is *meant by* "the mind enters into the object"!

However, with this (reasonably serious) caveat, this is a very useful book, because once one gets past (or skims over) the *technical jargon*, it is, as intended, a very detailed "road map" to what Vajrayana Buddhism is, coming from one whose opinions on the matter could certainly be held to be definitive! As I noted above, this would have been a VERY good book for me to have read prior to my first Kalachakra Initiation (Madison, 1981), as I sort of stumbled into Vajrayana by way of these major public events (I've taken the Kalachakra 3 times, and the Avalokitesvara twice), without much background knowledge other than basic College Religion Major data regarding Buddhism in general.

The Opening of the Wisdom Eye[3] is still in print, so if you were so inclined, you'd likely be able to get it through your local book retailer, but Amazon has it at a very reasonable discount price, and their new/used vendors have "like new" copies under three bucks. Again, this is awfully *technical*, but is quite a valuable addition to any Buddhist studies collection!

Notes:

1. http://btripp-books.livejournal.com/26274.html
2-3. http://amzn.to/2cd1Vgm

Tuesday, November 28, 2006[1]

Catching up ...

Yeah, I know, *two* book reviews on the same date, what *is* this world coming to? I figured that I'd cover this now, as it was a very quick read, and came out of the same stack as the last book. This is also a bit odd in that I can't find anything about it on the web ... although I did find a page with info on the author, Lopön Tenzin Namdak. I'm also not 100% sure about the title, but I think it ought to be Tapihritsa: The Condensed Meaning of an Explanation of the Teachings of Yungdrung Bon[2]. The booklet is one of those "Asian" formats that seems to be hand-set with actual metal type, with newsprint interior pages, and not a whole lot of publication info. Oddly enough, this was printed no earlier than 1991 as the translator's note in the book is dated from May of that year ... looking at it you'd guess it had been made decades ago, but I guess that's Kathmandu for ya. In the links that I would usually have going out to Amazon, I've targeted ~~the English language top page of yungdrung-bon.net,~~ *{since replaced by Shenten Dargye Ling[3]}* which has info on Lopön Tenzin Namdak ~~and is run by the Paris-based Yungdrung Bön Association~~ .

Now, if you're not familiar with it, Bön is the native "shamanistic" religion of Tibet, that strongly influenced the way that Vajrayana developed. I suspect that I picked this up at the NYC Kalachakra just to get some info on the Bönpo traditions. Frankly, though, I have a hard time really separating what's in this volume with the general stuff I've been exposed to of Vajrayana teachings. Perhaps Bönpo has become so intertwined with the Tibetan Buddhist lineages, that it has become something of a "heretical" close cousin, something like Sufism to mainstream Islam. Most of the materials that I can find on the web refer to it as the "Bön Buddhist tradition", which confuses me somewhat, as Bön is a survival from the *pre-Buddhist* times in Tibet.

Anyway, this is a fascinating little book ... it does, however, read very much like the last one in that there are a lot of things being "defined" in terms that are themselves *technical* and don't necessarily make things clear for the "outsider" reading it! Maybe some day I'll find a nice over-view book of the history (and survival) of Bön to get me up to speed with the subject. As noted, I was unable to find any source for this, so if you have a hankering for a copy, you're pretty much out of luck, although there do seem to be some decent basic web pages (http://bonpo.net/, http://www.bonfoundation.org/, etc.) with good info if you're interested in checking it out.

Notes:

1. http://btripp-books.livejournal.com/26470.html
2. https://goo.gl/Bycjn2
3. http://shenten.org/

Thursday, November 30, 2006[1]

A fabulous read ...

Well, this was a treat ... if you've been following along in this space, you'd know that I'd been sort of bitching about a number of these Tibetan books not quite getting around to defining *what* they were talking about, at least outside of a very technical set of images. Well, Chögyam Trungpa's Crazy Wisdom[2] avoids this quite nicely by being structured as a lecture-with-questions, so many of the things that a reader would be confused with are addressed in the Q&A section.

This book, while posthumously published in 1991 (Trungpa died in '87), actually dates to a series of lectures that he had done in the U.S. in 1972 dealing with the famed teacher Padmasambhava and the "Crazy Wisdom" approach to enlightenment. Chögyam Trungpa was, perhaps, an ideal figure to be introducing Vajrayana to the states at that time. A *tülku*, or re-incarnate Lama, he had come up via the traditional Tibetan monastic system, but at age 19 he had to flee the communist Chinese invasion, eventually, in his twenties, attending Oxford and there becoming fluent both in English and in the cognitive approaches of the West. Following this, he retreated to a period of solitary meditation at a monastery in Bhutan, an experience which dramatically changed him, as when he emerged from this period of isolation he opted to live as a secular person (as opposed to being a Monk), although still teaching. Soon after he moved to the U.S., married, and began his rather remarkable career of teaching, publication, and the founding of centers (including Naropa University in Boulder, CO). This book is an artifact of his early years here.

The subject of these lectures, Padmasambhava (the teacher who brought Buddhism to Tibet), is a remarkable figure, having eight "manifestations", each with a different name and attributes ... this allows Trungpa to break down his teachings into fairly easily-digestible bits, followed by questions by his students. The book is able, in this way, to transmit a great deal of the "crazy wisdom" approach that Trungpa sought to teach (along with his concept of "cutting through spiritual materialism") without bogging down in a lot of Tibetan technical terminology (although this is certainly *referenced*).

I was fortunate to be able to attend one of Chögyam Trungpa's lectures in the 80's, and he was at that point a "very complicated" figure. In his later years (he died at age 47), he was drinking very heavily, and was often (as in the case of the event I attended) quite late arriving for talks ... however, once in the "teaching mode" he was very direct, almost as though he was using the booze to "curtain off" all distractions so that what focus he had was purely on transmitting the dharma. Crazy Wisdom[3], however, dates from his prime, and I think it is the most accessible of his books (and I have read another half a dozen or so).

Unfortunately, it appears that Crazy Wisdom[4] is no longer in print, so you're going to have to rely on the "aftermarket" sellers for a copy. The good news is that you can get a *new* copy for about ten bucks (half of the original cover price), a "like new" copy for around five bucks, and a "good" copy for around a buck via the Amazon new/used vendors. Again, if you have *any* interest in Vajrayana, I would recommend this book ... while it is not "official" Vajrayana the way that the Dalai Lama's The Opening of the Wisdom Eye[5] is, reading it will certainly leave you less confused and a whole lot more inspired about what this path can accomplish!

Notes:

1. http://btripp-books.livejournal.com/26808.html

2-4. http://amzn.to/2bT6zSG

5. http://btripp-books.livejournal.com/26274.html

Friday, December 8, 2006[1]

hmmm ...

This was an odd one ... and I'm still not sure of the "why" of it. I mean, sure, collecting bits and pieces of wildly divergent "sacred prose" is all well and good, but ... it just seems *random*. Stephen Mitchell's editorial project, The Enlightened Mind: An Anthology of Sacred Prose[2] lacks any obvious (at least to my reading) unifying theme, or even a particular "axe to grind". Its Foreword indicates that it's the companion volume to "The Enlightened Heart", which perhaps has more editorializing involved, but this book, standing alone, has a bit of that "Readers Digest" feel of stuff stuck in because it filled the space. My more cynical (and former publisher) self was positing that Mr. Mitchell desperately wanted to "write" a "Deep Book" and found that the most expeditious way of doing this was to cobble together a bunch of pre-certified "Deep Stuff"!

Now, this is not to say that it's a *bad* book, or that it's not a useful little collection, or that it totally lacks structure. It is interesting in that it forms a timeline of ... what? ... *enlightened thought?* ... going from a two-page (!) excerpt from *The Upanishads*, followed by two pages or so of brief quotes from *The Bible*, through several dozen 1-10 page bits of various teachers, sages, prophets, books, and Smart Folks from all over the world. Ironically (for those paying close attention to my recent reviews here), both Padmasambhava and Franz Kafka make it into the book ... as do Jesus, Mohammad, Plato, and William Blake, with various Buddhist, Jewish, Moslem, Christian, and other teachers and theorists ... heck, even Albert Einstein gets a page of quotes.

Mitchell tosses off a brief introduction to each (ranging from 3 words to a half a page, with no particular attention given to the likelihood of any general reader recognizing the sage in question), but doesn't seem to make any effort to tie things together. Again, being exposed to a wide spectrum of "enlightened" writing is not a *bad thing*, certainly, but the take-away is a bit like having been handed a manila folder full of blurry xeroxes by some unstable person on the bus ... you're sure they're meaningful to *them*, but what's it supposed to mean *to me*?

I suppose that if one were, say, an accountant whose reading background was 99% economic and business books, this could be a goldmine if one was seeking out something more genteel to discuss over hors d'oeuvres with folks one wished to give the impression of being a more rounded person. For those of us with Liberal Arts degrees, however, it seems a bit pointless (O.K., except to perhaps introduce us to certain obscure-to-the-mainstream thinkers that we managed to not read on our own).

Remarkably, The Enlightened Mind[3] is still in print (so much for *my* publishing instincts!), so you could probably find it via your local bookstore, but you can also snag a used copy from the Amazon new/used vendors for around a buck. By the way, it looks like I'm going to make my "72 Books Read in 2006" target ... this was #69, and I'm a few dozen pages away from finishing up #70, and am starting in on #71 later today! Go me!

Notes:

1. http://btripp-books.livejournal.com/26913.html

2-3. http://amzn.to/2bT7hiB

Sunday, December 10, 2006[1]

an interesting read ...

This is another of those books that's been sitting around on my to-be-read shelves for over 15 years ... I guess the wheels of anthropology turn slower than those of subatomic particle physics, but I wonder how much of the info in this 1990 release is still current, especially the bits about genetic tracing.

Brian M. Fagan's The Journey from Eden: The Peopling of Our World[2] has a pretty direct premise, looking at the spread of humanity from its origins in sub-Saharan Africa and out into the various niches we currently occupy (for instance, whereas "anatomically modern humans" were in the Middle East as early as 100,000 years ago, remote places like New Zealand were only populated in the past 1,000 years!). The book largely walks through a timeline, looking at geological, archaeological, and anthropological information for various areas and discussing how various related/ancestor races (*Homo erectus*, Neanderthal, etc.) may have been supplanted by "modern man" (*Homo sapiens sapiens*).

This question is muddied by there being *two* competing general theories of the rise/spread of Humanity, one, the "candelabra theory" suggests that modern humans evolved separately from distinct groups of *Homo erectus* which had migrated out of Africa some one million years ago, leading to significant differences between African, European, and Asian peoples, the other, the "Noah's Ark" theory holds that modern humans evolved in Africa alone, and spread out to the rest of the world starting about 100,000 years ago, replacing (out-competing) our earlier, less clever (non-verbal/symbolic) cousins in the various environments around the world.

I suspect that, with the advances of genome mapping, many answers are currently available for questions posed in this book. Fagan does discuss the "Eve" mitochondrial data which indicates that all humans share a common female ancestor somewhere around 200,000 years ago (which would seem to favor the "Noah's Ark" distribution version), but I'm assuming more work has been done on this in the intervening time. It appears that the "population bottleneck" research post-dated this book ... this is DNA mapping which indicates that there was a significant population crash in ancestral Human stock somewhere around 70,000 years ago, at which point there were as few as *one thousand* surviving *Homo sapiens* (in the wake of a global environmental disaster brought about by a "supervolcano" eruption in Indonesia at that time which ejected something like 2,000 times the amount of ash into the atmosphere than the 1980 eruption of Mt. St. Helens) from whom we're all descended. In any event, I suspect that *some* of the arguments discussed here are by this point moot, based on more recent research.

The book has quite a lot of illustrations, from maps showing distribution of archaeological sites to drawings of various fossil remains, etc., most interesting of which are side-by-side comparisons of *Homo sapiens sapiens* with preceding forms of man, and diagrams of comparative stone-flaking "technologies" and "tool kits".

With the caveat that much of the research referred to in it may be out of date at this point, I'd heartily recommend The Journey from Eden[3] to anybody looking for a nice look into the early history of our species. The book walks a nice balance between disciplines (i.e. it does not get bogged down in dig details when discussing sites, and provides interesting parallels for ancient technologies in various cultures in the modern world), and keeps things moving at a decent pace. The book does appear to be out of print at this point, so you'd be looking at using the new/used vendors, and via Amazon there are "very good" copies for as little as 1¢, and a "new" copy for under $5.00 (not bad for a hardcover that had a $22.50 cover price back in 1990!), and either of those options would be well worth the investment to have this in your library.

Notes:

1. http://btripp-books.livejournal.com/27169.html

2-3. http://amzn.to/2bK2sqf

Monday, December 11, 2006

Very nice ...

As opposed to most of the books reviewed in this space of late, I only recently (in the past couple of weeks) bought this one. I'd been surfing through Amazon's *"recommended for you"* listings and noticed it. Now, I've read a good deal of the "Fourth Way" material, and have another half a dozen books by Ouspensky on my shelves, so I was surprised that I had never encountered (so that I'd noticed) his book on the Tarot, from either my readings of his writings, or my readings of material dealing with the Tarot.

So, I was very pleased to find that P.D. Ouspensky's The Symbolism of the Tarot: Philosophy of Occultism in Pictures and Numbers was quite a special little book. Now, I'm using "little" advisedly, as it is only 63 pages long, but it is quite an eye-opener. The first quarter of the book is Ouspensky's essay *about* the Tarot, and his discussion there is one of the clearest and most cogent of any that I've encountered (if bearing the "theosophical" slant of his age). I've always admired Ouspenksy's writing, as he takes the time to make sure that his readers are *following* what he's meaning to communicate (which is a highly unusual stance for most "metaphysical" authors!), and that's certainly evident in this essay.

The bulk of the book, however, are *meditations* on the Major Arcana. It appears that Ouspensky was working with the Rider-Waite deck, as his descriptions hew closely to these images. The cards are "read" in an interesting order ... starting at either end and alternating as he worked towards the middle (I, 0, II, XXI, III, XX, etc.), which corresponds to how he posits these archetypes being used in ancient mystery schools.

I was fascinated to discover things, via his descriptions, that I had *never noticed* in decades of familiarity with these cards (as an example, the reappearance of the towers from The Moon card in the background of the Death card), and found his "character development" imagery (that the Magician, the Fool, and the driver of the Chariot are all the same person at different stages, and that various women represent the unveiling of Nature and/or the Goddess through the mystical quest) very compelling.

Again, the combination of the discursive essay with the progressive meditations on the various cards ended up being quite a satisfying expression. Frankly, it almost seems out of character for Ouspensky to be dealing with something on this level, so it also has that "look for what seems out of place" element to it. This is hardly a standard Tarot book, but is more aligned to the sub-title "Philosophy of Occultism in Pictures and Numbers" embodied in Ouspensky's take on this one esoteric subject.

The present edition of Ouspensky's The Symbolism of the Tarot is a Dover 1976 reprint of the 1913 original (with the addition of the cover being a foldout that is printed both sides with copies of the Rider-Waite deck's Major Arcana, so that the reader can "follow along"), and is still in print for a very minimal $4.95 cover price ... although I picked it up for a buck via one of the Amazon new/used vendors. At this price, *everybody* with an interest in mysticism, the Tarot, or Ouspensky should definitely have this one in their library!

Notes:

1. http://btripp-books.livejournal.com/27399.html
2-3. http://amzn.to/2bT7gLw

Wednesday, December 20, 2006[1]

Eh, might as well get this review done too ...

Wheee ... look at that, I'm reviewing a book on the very same day I finished it ... How *efficient* of me! Frankly, I sort of want to get this out of the way, not only for reasons soon to become obvious, but with this I've reached my goal of having read 72 books in 2006. Whoopie! Now I can plow into some of those 600-page monsters that I've been putting off.

Ram Dass & Mirabai Bush's Compassion In Action: Setting Out on the Path of Service[2] is one of those books that's been sitting around on my to-be-read shelves since the early 90's, and, to be honest, I have NO idea why I bought this, or even why I ended up slotting it into my reading queue. I have gotten some *very* strange looks from my family when they've seen me reading this ... Shah, they understand, Castaneda, they expect, Crowley they assume, but they see me with "Compassion in Action" and act like I've had a stroke or something! I must admit, I had certain trepidations when picking this up, because my tolerance for "newagey" treacle is notably minimal, but it ended up being far better than I'd feared.

Actually, the *first half* of Compassion In Action[3] is quite fascinating, being something of a "spiritual memoir" by Ram Dass, covering several recollections that I'm sure were not easy for the former Dr. Richard Alpert to write about! In this part of the book Ram Dass takes a look at how he did or did not have compassion, or "heart connection" in various situations through his life, and how assorted unusual events moved him towards a more compassionate stance. Lovely stuff, and reasonably inspiring.

The second half of the book, however, is handed over to Mirabai Bush, who seems to be a "professional do-gooder" with all the newagey Leftist baggage that one would expect. I suppose that it is to her credit that the first 2/3rds of her part of the book at least *tries* to present a balanced look at "the path of action" (with sections that look at *why* people become activists, and the judgment errors so often involved in "well meaning" action, etc.). However, the last 50 pages of the book might as well be called (to borrow Lenin's phrase) "How To Be A 'Useful Idiot'" with advocacy for the worst sorts of anti-Western, anti-American, anti-sanity Leftist troublemaking. I suppose that the book saving the moonbattery for the last 15% of its duration was far better that what I *expected* going in, but it does drag what had been an engaging read down into the muck. If you stop reading about page 245, it's an O.K. book, if you persist through 299, it's abysmal.

Needless to say, Compassion In Action[4] is not something that I would particularly recommend, unless one is looking for more material on Ram Dass. Inexplicably, this is still in print, so might be lurking around your local bookstore, but "like new" copies of the hardcover edition can be had via Amazon's new/used vendors for as little as 25¢ ... and I would certainly advise going that route if for some reason you felt a need of adding this one to your library!

Notes:
1. http://btripp-books.livejournal.com/27790.html   2-4. http://amzn.to/2ccSDB6

QR code links to the on-line reviews:

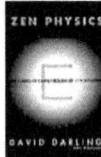

Zen Physics:
The Science of Death, the Logic of Reincarnation
by
David J. Darling

The Tao of Pooh
by
Benjamin Hoff

The Te of Piglet
by
Benjamin Hoff

Treason: Liberal Treachery
from the Cold War to the War on Terrorism
by
Ann Coulter

Slander:
Liberal Lies About the American Right
by
Ann Coulter

Breaking the Maya Code
by
Michael D. Coe

The Light at the Edge of the Universe:
Leading Cosmologists on the Brink
of a Scientific Revolution
by
Michael D. Lemonick

All The Trouble In The World: The Lighter Side
of Overpopulation, Famine, Ecological
Disaster, Ethnic Hatred, Plague, and Poverty
by
P.J. O'Rourke

God Is Red: A Native View of Religion
by
Vine Deloria, Jr.

Neuromancer
by
William Gibson

Parliament of Whores: A Lone Humorist
Attempts to Explain the Entire U.S. Government
by
P.J. O'Rourke

The Edges of Science:
Crossing the Boundary from Physics to Metaphysics
by
Richard Morris

Cosmic Coincidences:
Dark Matter, Mankind, and Anthropic Cosmology
by
John Gribbin & Martin Rees

Songs of the Doomed:
More Notes on the Death of the American Dream
by
Dr. Hunter S. Thompson

Why the Reckless Survive:
And Other Secrets of Human Nature
by
Melvin Konner

Fork It Over:
The Intrepid Adventures of a Professional Eater
by
Alan Richman

The Lost Ship of Noah:
In Search of the Ark at Ararat
by
Charles Berlitz

The Essential Kabbalah:
The Heart of Jewish Mysticism
by
Daniel C. Matt

Universes
by
John Leslie

Bible Code II: The Countdown
by
Michael Drosnin

The Mythology of North America
by
John Bierhorst

The Mythology of South America
by
John Bierhorst

The Mythology of Mexico and Central America
by
John Bierhorst

Weird Illinois
by
Troy Taylor

Voices Of The First Day:
Awakening In The Aboriginal Dreamtime
by
Robert Lawlor

You Are the World:
An Authentic Report of Talks
and Discussions in American Universities
by
J. Krishnamurti

When The Sun Moves Northward:
The Way Of Initiation
by
Mabel Collins

Creative Visualization:
Use the Power of Your Imagination
to Create What You Want in Your Life
by
Shakti Gawain

The Dervishes Of Turkey
by
Lucy M.J. Garnett

Voices Of Our Ancestors:
Cherokee Teachings from the Wisdom Fire
by
Dhyani Ywahoo

Eduardo El Curandero:
The Words of a Peruvian Healer
by
Douglas Sharon

The Dead Sea Scrolls: After Forty Years
by
Hershel Shanks

Unfit For Command:
Swift Boat Veterans Speak Out Against John Kerry
by
John E. O'Neill & Jerome R. Corsi

Get In The Van: On The Road With Black Flag
by
Henry Rollins

A Preliminary Edition Of The Unpublished
Dead Sea Scrolls: The Hebrew And Aramaic
Texts From Cave Four - Fascicle One
by
Ben Zion Wacholder

At the Heart of the Web:
The Inevitable Genesis of Intelligent Life
by
George A. Seielstad

Jesus & the Riddle of the Dead Sea Scrolls
by
Barbara Thiering

Reading the Mind of God:
In Search of the Principle of Universality
by
James Trefil

Stones, Bones, and Ancient Cities
by
Lawrence H. Robbins

The Pagan Book of Days
by
Nigel Pennick

Sufi Thought and Action
by
Idries Shah

Urban Legends and the Japanese Tale
by
David Schaefer

A Global Ethic: The Declaration
of the Parliament of the World's Religions
by
Hans Kung & Karl-Josef Kuschel

The Art of Napping
by
William A. Anthony

Mount Analogue: A Novel of Symbolically Authentic
Non-Euclidean Adventures in Mountain Climbing
by
Rene Daumal

Cultural Encounters: Essays on the Interactions
of Diverse Cultures Now and in the Past
by
Robert Cecil & David Wade, eds.

Archaeological Mexico
by
Marcia Castro Leal

Lost Kingdoms of the Maya
by
Gene S. Stuart & George E. Stuart

Sacred Architecture
by
A.T. Mann

The Secret Language of Symbols:
A Visual Key to Symbols and Their Meanings
by
David Fontana

Magick, Shamanism & Taoism:
The I Ching in Ritual and Meditation
by
Richard Herne

Kingdoms of Gold, Kingdoms of Jade:
The Americas Before Columbus
by
Brian M. Fagan

The New Archaeology and the Ancient Maya
by
Jeremy A. Sabloff

A Book of Angels
by
Sophy Burnham

Angel Letters
by
Sophy Burnham

The Gospel of Thomas:
The Hidden Sayings of Jesus
by
Marvin Meyer

Native American History:
A Chronology of a Culture's Vast Achievements
and Their Links to World Events
by
Judith Nies

Easy Field Guide to Southwestern Petroglyphs
by Elizabeth C. Welsh
Easy Field Guide to Indian Art & Legends of the Southwest
by James R. Cunkle
Easy Field Guide to Rock Art Symbols of the Southwest
by Rick Harris

Children of Kali:
Through India in Search of Bandits,
the Thug Cult, and the British Raj
by
Kevin Rushby

Meister Eckhart: A Modern Translation
by
Raymond B. Blakney

The Constitution of the United States
by
Harold J. Spaeth

Pagan Celtic Ireland:
The Enigma of the Irish Iron Age
by
Barry Raftery

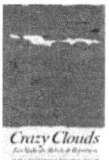

Crazy Clouds:
Zen Radicals, Rebels & Reformers
by
Perle Besserman & Manfred Steger

King, Warrior, Magician, Lover:
Rediscovering the Archetypes
of the Mature Masculine
by
Robert Moore & Douglas Gillette

Tao Te Ching:
The Classic Book of Integrity and the Way by Lao Tzu
by
Victor H. Mair

Stranger Music: Selected Poems and Songs
by
Leonard Cohen

The UFO Experience: A Scientific Inquiry
by
J. Allen Hynek

The Most Haunted House in England:
Ten Years' Investigation of Borley Rectory
by
Harry Price

Hidden Channels of the Mind
by
Louisa E. Rhine

The Road Ahead
by
Bill Gates

Between Bites:
Memoirs of a Hungry Hedonist
by
James Villas

The Celts: Europe's People of Iron
by
Dale M. Brown, Ed.

Aztecs: Reign of Blood and Splendor
by
Dale M. Brown, Ed.

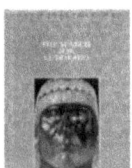

The Search For El Dorado
by
Dale M. Brown, Ed.

Egypt: Land of the Pharaohs
by
Dale M. Brown, Ed.

Ancient Egypt
by
John Baines & Jaromir Malek

Adventures in Afghanistan
by
Louis Palmer

My Life: From Brigand to King
-- Auto-biography of Amir Habibullah
by
Amir Habibullah & Jamal Gul

My Khyber Marriage
by
Morag Murray Abdulah

Afghan Caravan
by
Safia Shah, Ed.

Why Ireland Never Invaded America
by
Conor Cunneen

Prehistoric Mesoamerica
by
Richard E.W. Adams

Professional Hypnotism Manual:
A Practical Approach for Modern Times
by
John G. Kappas, Ph.D.

How to Talk to a Liberal (If You Must):
The World According to Ann Coulter
by
Ann Coulter

Tikal: A Handbook of the Ancient Maya Ruins
by
William R. Coe

A Forest of Kings:
The Untold Story of the Ancient Maya
by
Linda Schele & David Freidel

The Commanding Self
by
Idries Shah

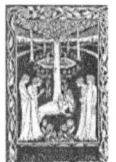

The Prophet Returns
by
Gunther Schaule

What Survives?:
Contemporary Explorations of Life After Death
by
Gary Doore, Ed.

Hyperspace: A Scientific Odyssey
through Parallel Universes, Time Warps,
and the Tenth Dimension
by
Michio Kaku

The Power of Silence: Further Lessons of Don Juan
by
Carlos Castaneda

The Teachings of Don Carlos:
Practical Applications of the Works
of Carlos Castaneda
by
Victor Sanchez

An Unlikely Prophet:
A Metaphysical Memoir
by the Legendary Writer of Superman and Batman
by
Alvin Schwartz

Flow: The Psychology of Optimal Experience
by
Mihaly Csikszentmihalyi

The Eagle's Gift
by
Carlos Castaneda

The Fire from Within
by
Carlos Castaneda

The Book of J
by
David Rosenberg & Harold Bloom

The God Particle:
If the Universe Is the Answer, What Is the Question?
by
Leon Lederman & Dick Teresi

The Opening of the Wisdom Eye
by
His Holiness the Dalai Lama, Tenzin Gyatso

Tapihritsa:
The Condensed Meaning of an Explanation
of the Teachings of Yungdrung Bon
by
Lopön Tenzin Namdak

Crazy Wisdom
by
Chögyam Trungpa

The Enlightened Mind: An Anthology of Sacred Prose
by
Stephen Mitchell

The Journey from Eden:
The Peopling of Our World
by
Brian M. Fagan

The Symbolism of the Tarot:
Philosophy of Occultism in Pictures and Numbers
by
P.D. Ouspensky

Compassion In Action:
Setting Out on the Path of Service
by
Ram Dass & Mirabai Bush

CONTENTS - ALPHABETICAL BY AUTHOR

Morag Murray Abdulah   page 127
    My Khyber Marriage

Richard E.W. Adams   page 132
    Prehistoric Mesoamerica

William A. Anthony   page 70
    The Art of Napping

John Baines & Jaromir Malek   page 121
    Ancient Egypt

Charles Berlitz   page 28
    The Lost Ship of Noah: In Search of the Ark at Ararat

Perle Besserman & Manfred Steger   page 100
    Crazy Clouds: Zen Radicals, Rebels & Reformers

John Bierhorst   page 35
    The Mythology of Mexico and Central America

John Bierhorst   page 33
    The Mythology of North America

John Bierhorst   page 34
    The Mythology of South America

Raymond B. Blakney   page 95
    Meister Eckhart: A Modern Translation

Harold Bloom & David Rosenberg *The Book of J*	page	157
Dale M. Brown, Ed. *Aztecs: Reign of Blood and Splendor*	page	118
Dale M. Brown, Ed. *Egypt: Land of the Pharaohs*	page	120
Dale M. Brown, Ed. *The Celts: Europe's People of Iron*	page	117
Dale M. Brown, Ed. *The Search For El Dorado*	page	119
Sophy Burnham *Angel Letters*	page	86
Sophy Burnham *A Book of Angels*	page	85
Eduardo Calderon & Douglas Sharon *Eduardo El Curandero: The Words of a Peruvian Healer*	page	46
Carlos Castaneda *The Eagle's Gift*	page	154
Carlos Castaneda *The Fire from Within*	page	155
Carlos Castaneda *The Power of Silence: Further Lessons of Don Juan*	page	149

Robert Cecil & David Wade, eds.   page 72
Cultural Encounters: Essays on the Interactions of Diverse Cultures Now and in the Past

Michael D. Coe   page 10
Breaking the Maya Code

William R. Coe   page 138
Tikal: A Handbook of the Ancient Maya Ruins

Leonard Cohen   page 105
Stranger Music: Selected Poems and Songs

Mabel Collins   page 40
When The Sun Moves Northward: The Way Of Initiation

Ann Coulter   page 136
How to Talk to a Liberal (If You Must): The World According to Ann Coulter

Ann Coulter   page 9
Slander: Liberal Lies About the American Right

Ann Coulter   page 7
Treason: Liberal Treachery from the Cold War to the War on Terrorism

Mihaly Csikszentmihalyi   page 153
Flow: The Psychology of Optimal Experience

James R. Cunkle   page 91
Easy Field Guide to Indian Art & Legends of the Southwest

Conor Cunneen — page 131
Why Ireland Never Invaded America

His Holiness the Dalai Lama, Tenzin Gyatso — page 160
The Opening of the Wisdom Eye

David J. Darling — page 4
Zen Physics: The Science of Death, the Logic of Reincarnation

Ram Dass & Mirabai Bush — page 171
Compassion In Action: Setting Out on the Path of Service

Rene Daumal — page 71
Mount Analogue: A Novel of Symbolically Authentic Non-Euclidean Adventures in Mountain Climbing

Vine Deloria, Jr. — page 14
God Is Red: A Native View of Religion

Gary Doore, Ed. — page 146
What Survives?: Contemporary Explorationsof Life After Death

Michael Drosnin — page 31
Bible Code II: The Countdown

Brian M. Fagan — page 82
Kingdoms of Gold, Kingdoms of Jade: The Americas Before Columbus

Brian M. Fagan — page 167
The Journey from Eden: The Peopling of Our World

David Fontana	page	78
The Secret Language of Symbols : A Visual Key to Symbols and Their Meanings		
Lucy M.J. Garnett	page	42
The Dervishes Of Turkey		
Bill Gates	page	113
The Road Ahead		
Shakti Gawain	page	41
Creative Visualization: Use the Power of Your Imagination to Create What You Want in Your Life		
William Gibson	page	16
Neuromancer		
John Gribbin & Martin Rees	page	20
Cosmic Coincidences: Dark Matter, Mankind, and Anthropic Cosmology		
Amir Habibullah & Jamal Gul	page	125
My Life: From Brigand to King -- Auto-biography of Amir Habibullah		
Rick Harris	page	91
Easy Field Guide to Rock Art Symbols of the Southwest		
Richard Herne	page	80
Magick, Shamanism & Taoism: The I Ching in Ritual and Meditation		
Benjamin Hoff	page	5
The Tao of Pooh		

Author	Title	Page
Benjamin Hoff	*The Te of Piglet*	6
J. Allen Hynek	*The UFO Experience: A Scientific Inquiry*	107
Michio Kaku	*Hyperspace: A Scientific Odyssey through Parallel Universes, Time Warps, and the Tenth Dimension*	147
John G. Kappas, Ph.D.	*Professional Hypnotism Manual: A Practical Approach for Modern Times*	134
Melvin Konner	*Why the Reckless Survive: And Other Secrets of Human Nature*	23
J. Krishnamurti	*You Are the World: An Authentic Report of Talks and Discussions in American Universities*	39
Hans Kung & Karl-Josef Kuschel	*A Global Ethic: The Declaration of the Parliament of the World's Religions*	68
Robert Lawlor	*Voices Of The First Day: Awakening In The Aboriginal Dreamtime*	37
Marcia Castro Leal	*Archaeological Mexico*	74
Leon Lederman & Dick Teresi	*The God Particle: If the Universe Is the Answer, What Is the Question?*	159

Michael D. Lemonick — page 12
The Light at the Edge of the Universe: Leading Cosmologists on the Brink of a Scientific Revolution

John Leslie — page 30
Universes

Victor H. Mair — page 103
Tao Te Ching: The Classic Book of Integrity and the Way by Lao Tzu

A.T. Mann — page 76
Sacred Architecture

Daniel C. Matt — page 29
The Essential Kabbalah: The Heart of Jewish Mysticism

Marvin Meyer — page 88
The Gospel of Thomas: The Hidden Sayings of Jesus

Stephen Mitchell — page 165
The Enlightened Mind: An Anthology of Sacred Prose

Robert Moore & Douglas Gillette — page 101
King, Warrior, Magician, Lover: Rediscovering the Archetypes of the Mature Masculine

Richard Morris — page 18
The Edges of Science: Crossing the Boundary from Physics to Metaphysics

Lopön Tenzin Namdak — page 162
Tapihritsa: The Condensed Meaning of an Explanation of the Teachings of Yungdrung Bon

Judith Nies   page 90
> *Native American History: A Chronology of a Culture's Vast Achievements and Their Links to World Events*

John E. O'Neill & Jerome R. Corsi   page 50
> *Unfit For Command: Swift Boat Veterans Speak Out Against John Kerry*

P.J. O'Rourke   page 13
> *All The Trouble In The World: The Lighter Side of Overpopulation, Famine, Ecological Disaster, Ethnic Hatred, Plague, and Poverty*

P.J. O'Rourke   page 17
> *Parliament of Whores: A Lone Humorist Attempts to Explain the Entire U.S. Government*

P.D. Ouspensky   page 169
> *The Symbolism of the Tarot: Philosophy of Occultism in Pictures and Numbers*

Louis Palmer   page 123
> *Adventures in Afghanistan*

Nigel Pennick   page 64
> *The Pagan Book of Days*

Harry Price   page 109
> *The Most Haunted House in England: Ten Years' Investigation of Borley Rectory*

Barry Raftery   page 99
> *Pagan Celtic Ireland: The Enigma of the Irish Iron Age*

Louisa E. Rhine   page 111
> *Hidden Channels of the Mind*

Alan Richman — page 27
Fork It Over: The Intrepid Adventures of a Professional Eater

Lawrence H. Robbins — page 63
Stones, Bones, and Ancient Cities

Henry Rollins — page 52
Get In The Van: On The Road With Black Flag

Kevin Rushby — page 93
Children of Kali: Through India in Search of Bandits, the Thug Cult, and the British Raj

Jeremy A. Sabloff — page 84
The New Archaeology and the Ancient Maya

Victor Sanchez — page 150
The Teachings of Don Carlos: Practical Applications of the Works of Carlos Castaneda

David Schaefer — page 67
Urban Legends and the Japanese Tale

Gunther Schaule — page 144
The Prophet Returns

Linda Schele & David Freidel — page 140
A Forest of Kings: The Untold Story of the Ancient Maya

Alvin Schwartz — page 151
An Unlikely Prophet: A Metaphysical Memoir by the Legendary Writer of Superman and Batman

George A. Seielstad   page 57
*At the Heart of the Web:
The Inevitable Genesis of Intelligent Life*

Safia Shah, Ed.   page 129
Afghan Caravan

Idries Shah   page 142
The Commanding Self

Idries Shah   page 65
Sufi Thought and Action

Hershel Shanks   page 48
The Dead Sea Scrolls: After Forty Years

Harold J. Spaeth   page 97
The Constitution of the United States

Gene S. Stuart & George E. Stuart   page 75
Lost Kingdoms of the Maya

Troy Taylor   page 36
Weird Illinois

Barbara Thiering   page 59
Jesus & the Riddle of the Dead Sea Scrolls

Dr. Hunter S. Thompson   page 22
*Songs of the Doomed:
More Notes on the Death of the American Dream*

James Trefil   page 61
*Reading the Mind of God:
In Search of the Principle of Universality*

Chögyam Trungpa   page 163
Crazy Wisdom

James Villas   page 115
Between Bites: Memoirs of a Hungry Hedonist

Ben Zion Wacholder   page 54
A Preliminary Edition Of The Unpublished Dead Sea Scrolls: The Hebrew And Aramaic Texts From Cave Four - Fascicle One

Elizabeth C. Welsh   page 91
Easy Field Guide to Southwestern Petroglyphs

Dhyani Ywahoo   page 44
Voices Of Our Ancestors: Cherokee Teachings from the Wisdom Fire

CONTENTS - ALPHABETICAL BY TITLE

Adventures in Afghanistan
Louis Palmer   page 123

Afghan Caravan
Safia Shah, Ed.   page 129

All The Trouble In The World:
The Lighter Side of Overpopulation, Famine, Ecological
Disaster, Ethnic Hatred, Plague, and Poverty
P.J. O'Rourke   page   13

Ancient Egypt
John Baines & Jaromir Malek   page 121

Angel Letters
Sophy Burnham   page   86

Archaeological Mexico
Marcia Castro Leal   page   74

The Art of Napping
William A. Anthony   page   70

At the Heart of the Web:
The Inevitable Genesis of Intelligent Life
George A. Seielstad   page   57

Aztecs: Reign of Blood and Splendor
Dale M. Brown, Ed.   page 118

Between Bites: Memoirs of a Hungry Hedonist
James Villas — page 115

Bible Code II: The Countdown
Michael Drosnin — page 31

A Book of Angels
Sophy Burnham — page 85

The Book of J
Harold Bloom & David Rosenberg — page 157

Breaking the Maya Code
Michael D. Coe — page 10

The Celts: Europe's People of Iron
Dale M. Brown, Ed. — page 117

Children of Kali: Through India in Search of Bandits, the Thug Cult, and the British Raj
Kevin Rushby — page 93

The Commanding Self
Idries Shah — page 142

Compassion In Action: Setting Out on the Path of Service
Ram Dass & Mirabai Bush — page 171

The Constitution of the United States
Harold J. Spaeth — page 97

Cosmic Coincidences: Dark Matter, Mankind, and Anthropic Cosmology
John Gribbin & Martin Rees — page 20

Crazy Clouds: Zen Radicals, Rebels & Reformers
Perle Besserman & Manfred Steger   page 100

Crazy Wisdom
Chögyam Trungpa   page 163

*Creative Visualization: Use the Power of Your
Imagination to Create What You Want in Your Life*
Shakti Gawain   page 41

*Cultural Encounters: Essays on the Interactions
of Diverse Cultures Now and in the Past*
Robert Cecil & David Wade, eds.   page 72

The Dead Sea Scrolls: After Forty Years
Hershel Shanks   page 48

The Dervishes Of Turkey
Lucy M.J. Garnett   page 42

The Eagle's Gift
Carlos Castaneda   page 154

*Easy Field Guide to Indian Art & Legends
of the Southwest*
James R. Cunkle   page 91

*Easy Field Guide to Rock Art Symbols
of the Southwest*
Rick Harris   page 91

Easy Field Guide to Southwestern Petroglyphs
Elizabeth C. Welsh   page 91

The Edges of Science: Crossing the Boundary from Physics to Metaphysics
Richard Morris — page 18

Eduardo El Curandero: The Words of a Peruvian Healer
Eduardo Calderon & Douglas Sharon — page 46

Egypt: Land of the Pharaohs
Dale M. Brown, Ed. — page 120

The Enlightened Mind: An Anthology of Sacred Prose
Stephen Mitchell — page 165

The Essential Kabbalah: The Heart of Jewish Mysticism
Daniel C. Matt — page 29

The Fire from Within
Carlos Castaneda — page 155

Flow: The Psychology of Optimal Experience
Mihaly Csikszentmihalyi — page 153

A Forest of Kings: The Untold Story of the Ancient Maya
Linda Schele & David Freidel — page 140

Fork It Over: The Intrepid Adventures of a Professional Eater
Alan Richman — page 27

Get In The Van: On The Road With Black Flag
Henry Rollins — page 52

*A Global Ethic: The Declaration
of the Parliament of the World's Religions*
Hans Kung & Karl-Josef Kuschel   page   68

God Is Red: A Native View of Religion
Vine Deloria, Jr.   page   14

*The God Particle:
If the Universe Is the Answer, What Is the Question?*
Leon Lederman & Dick Teresi   page 159

The Gospel of Thomas: The Hidden Sayings of Jesus
Marvin Meyer   page   88

Hidden Channels of the Mind
Louisa E. Rhine   page 111

*How to Talk to a Liberal (If You Must):
The World According to Ann Coulter*
Ann Coulter   page 136

*Hyperspace: A Scientific Odyssey through Parallel
Universes, Time Warps, and the Tenth Dimension*
Michio Kaku   page 147

Jesus & the Riddle of the Dead Sea Scrolls
Barbara Thiering   page   59

The Journey from Eden: The Peopling of Our World
Brian M. Fagan   page 167

*King, Warrior, Magician, Lover: Rediscovering
the Archetypes of the Mature Masculine*
Robert Moore & Douglas Gillette   page 101

Kingdoms of Gold, Kingdoms of Jade:
The Americas Before Columbus
Brian M. Fagan   page   82

The Light at the Edge of the Universe: Leading
Cosmologists on the Brink of a Scientific Revolution
Michael D. Lemonick   page   12

Lost Kingdoms of the Maya
Gene S. Stuart & George E. Stuart   page   75

The Lost Ship of Noah: In Search of the Ark at Ararat
Charles Berlitz   page   28

Magick, Shamanism & Taoism:
The I Ching in Ritual and Meditation
Richard Herne   page   80

Meister Eckhart: A Modern Translation
Raymond B. Blakney   page   95

The Most Haunted House in England:
Ten Years' Investigation of Borley Rectory
Harry Price   page   109

Mount Analogue: A Novel of Symbolically Authentic
Non-Euclidean Adventures in Mountain Climbing
Rene Daumal   page   71

My Khyber Marriage
Morag Murray Abdulah   page   127

My Life: From Brigand to King
-- Auto-biography of Amir Habibullah
Amir Habibullah & Jamal Gul   page   125

The Mythology of Mexico and Central America		
John Bierhorst	page	35
The Mythology of North America		
John Bierhorst	page	33
The Mythology of South America		
John Bierhorst	page	34
Native American History: A Chronology of a Culture's Vast Achievements and Their Links to World Events		
Judith Nies	page	90
Neuromancer		
William Gibson	page	16
The New Archaeology and the Ancient Maya		
Jeremy A. Sabloff	page	84
The Opening of the Wisdom Eye		
His Holiness the Dalai Lama, Tenzin Gyatso	page	160
The Pagan Book of Days		
Nigel Pennick	page	64
Pagan Celtic Ireland: The Enigma of the Irish Iron Age		
Barry Raftery	page	99
Parliament of Whores: A Lone Humorist Attempts to Explain the Entire U.S. Government		
P.J. O'Rourke	page	17
The Power of Silence: Further Lessons of Don Juan		
Carlos Castaneda	page	149

Prehistoric Mesoamerica
Richard E.W. Adams   page 132

*A Preliminary Edition Of The Unpublished
Dead Sea Scrolls: The Hebrew And Aramaic Texts
From Cave Four - Fascicle One*
Ben Zion Wacholder   page 54

*Professional Hypnotism Manual:
A Practical Approach for Modern Times*
John G. Kappas, Ph.D.   page 134

The Prophet Returns
Gunther Schaule   page 144

*Reading the Mind of God:
In Search of the Principle of Universality*
James Trefil   page 61

The Road Ahead
Bill Gates   page 113

Sacred Architecture
A.T. Mann   page 76

The Search For El Dorado
Dale M. Brown, Ed.   page 119

*The Secret Language of Symbols :
A Visual Key to Symbols and Their Meanings*
David Fontana   page 78

Slander: Liberal Lies About the American Right
Ann Coulter   page 9

Songs of the Doomed:
More Notes on the Death of the American Dream
Dr. Hunter S. Thompson   page   22

Stones, Bones, and Ancient Cities
Lawrence H. Robbins   page   63

Stranger Music: Selected Poems and Songs
Leonard Cohen   page 105

Sufi Thought and Action
Idries Shah   page   65

The Symbolism of the Tarot:
Philosophy of Occultism in Pictures and Numbers
P.D. Ouspensky   page 169

The Tao of Pooh
Benjamin Hoff   page   5

Tao Te Ching:
The Classic Book of Integrity and the Way by Lao Tzu
Victor H. Mair   page 103

The Te of Piglet
Benjamin Hoff   page   6

Tapihritsa: The Condensed Meaning of an Explanation
of the Teachings of Yungdrung Bon
Lopön Tenzin Namdak   page 162

The Teachings of Don Carlos: Practical Applications
of the Works of Carlos Castaneda
Victor Sanchez   page 150

Tikal: A Handbook of the Ancient Maya Ruins
William R. Coe   page 138

*Treason: Liberal Treachery
from the Cold War to the War on Terrorism*
Ann Coulter   page   7

The UFO Experience: A Scientific Inquiry
J. Allen Hynek   page 107

*Unfit For Command:
Swift Boat Veterans Speak Out Against John Kerry*
John E. O'Neill & Jerome R. Corsi   page 50

Universes
John Leslie   page 30

*An Unlikely Prophet: A Metaphysical Memoir
by the Legendary Writer of Superman and Batman*
Alvin Schwartz   page 151

Urban Legends and the Japanese Tale
David Schaefer   page 67

*Voices Of Our Ancestors:
Cherokee Teachings from the Wisdom Fire*
Dhyani Ywahoo   page 44

*Voices Of The First Day:
Awakening In The Aboriginal Dreamtime*
Robert Lawlor   page 37

Weird Illinois
Troy Taylor   page 36

What Survives?: Contemporary Explorations of Life After Death
Gary Doore, Ed. page 146

When The Sun Moves Northward: The Way Of Initiation
Mabel Collins page 40

Why Ireland Never Invaded America
Conor Cunneen page 131

Why the Reckless Survive: And Other Secrets of Human Nature
Melvin Konner page 23

You Are the World: An Authentic Report of Talks and Discussions in American Universities
J. Krishnamurti page 39

Zen Physics: The Science of Death, the Logic of Reincarnation
David J. Darling page 4

www.ingramcontent.com/pod-product-compliance
Lightning Source LLC
Chambersburg PA
CBHW071310110426
42743CB00042B/1243